D1568295

CHALLENGING THE
Mississippi
Firebombers

Jim Dann

CHALLENGING THE
Mississippi
Firebombers

Memories of Mississippi 1964-65

Baraka
Books
Montréal

ISBN 978-1-926824-87-1 pbk; 978-1-926824-89-5 epub; 978-1-926824-88-8 pdf; 978-1-926824-90-1 mobi/kindle

Cover photos: by Herschel Kaminsky: Otis Brown and Mckinley Mack lead the Freedom Day picket line at the Sunflower County Courthouse, January 4, 1965. UHURU means "Freedom" in Swahili.
Cartography by Julie Benoît
Cover by Folio infographie
Book design by Folio infographie

Herschel Kaminsky, photos: front and back covers: pp. 15, 27, 29, 30, 43, 59, 77, 88, 95, 103, 118, 129, 134, 136, 137, 167, 170, 171, 173, 174, 184

Mabel Giles Whitaker, photo p. 147

Rachel Dann, photos: pp. 82, 203, 212

Pamela Harris, photos: pp. 211, 213

Stacy White, photo: p. 82

Library of Congress, photo: p. 113 (permission requested)

Tracy Sugarman, illustrations: pp. 9, 33, 42, 55, 73, 79

© Baraka Books 2013
Legal Deposit, 3rd quarter 2013

Bibliothèque et Archives nationales du Québec
Library and Archives Canada

Published by Baraka Books of Montreal.
6977, rue Lacroix
Montréal, Québec H4E 2V4
Telephone: 514 808-8504
info@barakabooks.com
www.barakabooks.com

Trade Distribution & Returns
Canada and the United States
Independent Publishers Group
1-800-888-4741 (IPG1);
orders@ipgbook.com

Praise from around the world

"Many opposed slavery, but few were abolitionists; many opposed segregation, but few lifted a hand to end it. Jim Dann answered the call. If you want to know the how and why of fighting oppression, open this book."

Phil Taylor, Radio Broadcaster at CIUT, Toronto

"A very vivid account of extraordinary commitment and courage by young Americans to achieve what was perhaps the most important social change of our time."

Alan Perry, New Zealand

"In the early 1960s I was studying history at Auckland University in New Zealand. We were fascinated and somewhat horrified to follow what was happening in the US South to those who were working to enfranchise voters from the Black community. This was happening in a country that prided itself as being the leader of the democratic world. In 2012 a friend lent me an early copy of Jim Dann's memoirs. It was a riveting read. It is a vivid account from someone who had experienced the fight for the right of Blacks to vote rather than from someone who had read about it. I could not put it down until I had finished it and everyone in our household read it and had the same reaction. Even although it was about events that took place over fifty years ago in a country thousands of miles away it resonated with us all and triggered our memories of that time. Jim's story has raw emotion, suspense, courage, politics and friendship. What more could you want in a book?"

Anne Martin

To Charles McLaurin, who made it all possible.

To Aaron, Gabrielle, Elleora, Micol, Ashaan, Jaya:
it is time to tell these tales to the grandchildren.

My husband Jim was involved in many struggles during his lifetime, but he always told me that the work he did in Mississippi during 1964-65 was the most important and personally meaningful activity of his life. When Jim told stories from those fifteen months he was there, he spoke humbly of his role, and with immense admiration for the black citizenry who had been bravely struggling for years for basic human rights and equality. He was awed by how much they risked, welcoming and housing voter registration volunteers. He was impressed by the enthusiasm and commitment of young black teenagers and even primary school children. He felt he learned important lessons in leadership strategy and tactics, integrity and dignity, and persistence in the face of daunting odds from the veteran Mississippi SNCC leaders and also from the black citizenry and their enthusiastic children. This book is a tribute to their struggle and courage.

Jim was a brave, bold, enthusiastic man with a commitment to equality and fairness to the end of his life.

Arley DANN, July 15, 2013.

Table of Contents

List of Maps   12

Preface by John Harris   13

Introduction   15
  1. A Trip from Los Angeles to Ohio   19
  2. The Training in Oxford, Ohio   31
  3. Our Base in Ruleville   53
  4. The Standoff in Drew   73
  5. Breakthrough in Indianola   91
  6. The Autumn Desegregation Offensive in Indianola   121
  7. The Klan Strikes Back   141
  8. A Winter to Keep On Pushing   157
  9. New Hopes and New Paths of Struggle   179
10. Return to Mississippi   203

Afterword by John Harris   221

Appendix – Organizations and Civil Rights Leaders
Referred to   225

A Short Note on Sources   229

Acknowledgements   233

Publisher's Note   237

List of Maps

State of Mississippi 51

Sunflower County, Mississippi 52

Town of Indianola, Mississippi 89

Preface by John Harris

··

This is about a one-year experience in the mid-twentieth century United States (1964-1965).

It takes place in the state of Mississippi and involves many out-of-state students and other volunteers. It was led by individuals and a civil rights organization, the Student Nonviolent Coordinating Committee, SNCC, that only had a few years' experience.

The experience touched many brave and curious Mississippi citizens, both young and old, and covers some of the barriers set up by local county and state authorities to stop the changes they didn't want to see.

The right to vote was the main issue. But as the movement became more active and broader it challenged public accommodations, school segregation, law enforcement and police brutality.

Many of the student volunteers had never participated in any movement as intense as this—although some had other movement experience back home. The local Mississippi youth were new to these struggles and joined in strong numbers, although they were afraid and quiet in the beginning.

We saw local adults taking in volunteers to stay in their homes, going to register to vote, attending mass meetings, going to the Freedom Schools and doing things they had never done before.

The activities in Mississippi saw lots of support from individuals and groups around the country. Supporters helped to publicize the activities going on in the towns and counties. News of the arrests, brutality, mass meetings and house fires helped to mobilize support for those in the struggle with bail money, volunteer legal assistance and moral support.

Let's hope we learned lots of lessons from our experiences, and for those who are reminded of what happened and those who may be fairly new to these experiences, let's keep passing the lessons on. We can use lots of experience and thoughts on some of the challenges we face now!

John Harris (1943-2012)
January 2011

John Harris speaks to rally in Indianola on Freedom Day, January 4, 1965. John Harris organized the five-hundred-person subsequent picket line at the Courthouse. To his right in the tie is Bridges Randle, who organized a boycott of college students at Mississippi Valley State that day.

Introduction

···

This small essay was requested by some members of my family and thus, encouraged by them and also by my lifelong comrade and friend, the late John Harris, I put my memory to the test, and wrote down the following thoughts.

This is then definitely not a dispassionate history, simply a recounting of my memories of events now almost fifty years later. With the passage of time and my limited perspective, they are my personal memories and they obviously focus on events I was involved with and can be quite sketchy about other equally or more important events, which may have been occurring at the same time, even in Sunflower County. My primary source is then my memories, but names and dates get vague with the passage of years, and I wanted to be as accurate as possible so I consulted the memories of others, particularly John Harris, and I relied as much as possible for details on such primary sources such as reports from the Council of Federated Organizations (COFO), WATS (Wide Area Telephone Service) or the histories by the Sunflower County Black Historical Society. Sources are provided at the end of this essay.

My subtitle also should restrict me to the time I was actually in Mississippi. But I found it necessary to provide background on the history before my time in Mississippi, otherwise I am afraid young people today would find the situations I describe impossible to make sense of. These diversions have been kept as brief as possible since a few decent histories of the Civil War and Reconstruction times are now available and W.E.B. Dubois's masterly histories of that period are as pertinent today as ever.

Some readers may disagree with the view presented of some figures like John Kennedy, Hubert Humphrey and Lyndon Johnson, who are elsewhere portrayed as great supporters of the civil rights movement. In my view their support was at best restricted to the legislative and legal arenas, and as far as the active movement in the South was concerned their support had little beneficial effect. Please bear with me if this view offends. Also some may object to my lack of charity to our racist opponents, many now dead. I freely admit this fault, if it be one, but feel I have good reason.

Finally I found it helpful to focus my memories by including a phrase from Shakespeare before every chapter. These words, universally relevant, were helpful to me to come to grips with the powerful emotions these memories still evoke.

For today's young people it may be hard to visualize a society without computers, Internet, cell phones, social networks and the like; even telephones were often an expensive luxury; for example, in the town of Sunflower not a single black person had either phone service or television in 1964.

Discrimination against blacks was a nationwide disgrace in the fifties. There were large sections of cities like New York, Boston and Chicago into which blacks dared not enter even in daylight. I, growing up in liberal New England, never saw an interracial couple; California outlawed interracial marriage. Washington, DC, the capital of the "free world," had segregated schools, and as late as 1962-63 its surroundings in Maryland had hamburger chains, beaches and amusement parks to which blacks were not allowed entrance. Our "national pastime," baseball, excluded black players. As an eighteen-year-old Collier's Encyclopedia salesman in Rhode Island in 1958 I was expressly forbidden by my employer to sell to black people, no matter their economic status.

As one went south into the states of the old Confederacy everything was segregated, from public drinking fountains and restrooms to hotels and restaurants. From virtually all state and local government buildings flew the infamous battle flag of the slaveowners' rebellion, the Stars and Bars, often placed above that of the United States flag so as to emphasize the white rulers' defiant fidelity to racism even over country. Meanwhile newspapers and politicians routinely spewed the most disgustingly vile racist lies about their black citizens. As one entered the Deep South states at the South Carolina border blacks there encountered an incredibly humiliating system of racist insults and incivility in their daily life; so bad it was almost impossible for them to have any relationship even of business without being treated with total disrespect. Naturally voting rights and any participation in the political process in those states were denied blacks. Finally one came to the most benighted state of all, Mississippi, where murder of blacks for little or no reason was not at all an uncommon recreation for some of the more depraved white men, and even if the more respectable types disapproved, they never ever punished the murderers.

It was absolutely crucial to the politics of racism to have ideological underpinning in both a phony anthropology and a false history. There was bandied about in those days in many intellectual circles a perverse and totally unscientific "theory" of races, which ascribed to the white "race" some kind of superiority. These unsupported speculations of early twentieth-century pseudo-scientists became widespread by the 1950s and found their way into anthropology texts and popular encyclopedias, sometimes accompanied by shameful graphics and absurd generalizations. Even more pervasive in the "scholarly" world was a highly mendacious history of slavery and the Civil War, which was taught nationwide in both high school and college. The text in my 1963 history course at UCLA on the Civil War was written by a pair of Louisiana professors who made a mockery of the horrors of slavery and pilloried those who had fought racism. Treasonous generals like Robert E.

Lee were now universally admired heroes, while those who fought them, men like Ulysses S. Grant, Edwin Stanton or William Tecumseh Sherman, were the villains of this completely false but accepted "history." Particularly pilloried by the history writers of that decade were the 1865 pioneers of the civil rights ideals in Congress, men like Hiram Revels, William Sumner, Ben Butler and Thaddeus Stevens. All this rewriting of history had become accepted "fact" throughout the country. Network TV and writers of popular history like John F. Kennedy swallowed this sophistry hook, line and sinker, and recycled the myths of this history onto the general public as in Kennedy's book *Profiles in Courage.*

In opposition to the discriminatory political system with its ideological support a group of young men and women had been working for a decade for civil rights.[1] This then is the setting of *My Memories of Mississippi.*

---

1. A short list of organizations and leaders is provided in the Appendix.

1

A Trip from Los Angeles to Ohio

··

There is a tide in the affairs of men,
Which taken at the flood leads on to fortune;
Omitted all the voyage of their life
Is bound in shallows and in miseries.
On such a full sea we are now afloat,
And we must take the current when it serves
Or lose our ventures.

Julius CAESAR

In June 1964 I found myself in a small, green, overcrowded Buick crossing the country from Los Angeles to the southern Ohio town of Oxford, where the training for the 1964 Freedom Summer was about to take place. The Mississippi Voter Registration Project had indeed been bound in shallows and miseries for some time now. Through state-sanctioned murders, beatings, jailings and arson very few black voters had been able to register. But in the country as a whole a rising tide of energy and determination was percolating on all the major college campuses. The time was ripe to pit the energy and idealism of progressive students against the obstinacy of official Mississippi. Bob Moses, who for three years had been leading the struggle in that state, saw the opportunity and convinced his comrades on the front lines that a bold new approach was needed, that they must take the current despite the enormous risks.

We were not the first idealistic Northerners to head south to join the struggle for equality being led by black Mississippians. A hundred years before, Northerners, derisively called "Carpetbaggers," had entered Mississippi during the period known as Reconstruction to build the most democratic society this country had ever seen. This period was authoritatively and massively documented by the historian W.E.B. Dubois.

The owner of the car was a UCLA student whose name I don't remember. He went home after half of the Ohio training, and I never saw him again. The second passenger was Ron Ridenour, my housemate in Venice, California, at 412 Carroll Canal. I was the third. The rest of the car was filled to the roof with donated clothing that Ron had collected from Los Angeles radicals and socialists for the people of Mississippi who had been evicted from their plantations for daring to register to vote. I met Ron and first heard about the Mississippi summer project in the W.E.B. Dubois Club of UCLA.

In the fall of 1963 I took an advanced historiography class at UCLA as part of my graduate program. We were supposed to pick one historian and write a research paper on him. I decided to pick W.E.B. Dubois since I wanted to know more about the most famous black historian. As it turned out there were two young women in the class who were leftists. They seemed to have been worried about my pick since Dubois had joined the Communist Party at the end of his life and they feared I would trash him for it. So one of them approached the professor and asked if she could also do Dubois, to counter my anticipated anti-communist view. She got permission from the progressive professor but did a shallow, poorly researched panegyric. Much to my classmates' surprise when it was my time to give my report, which was heavily researched and well documented, they found me fully sympathetic to Dubois and his perspective on the history of slavery and Reconstruction. Nor did I fault him for joining the Communist Party, given his academic background and FBI persecution in the fifties. Dubois died in exile in Ghana in 1963.

The young women then asked me to join the Dubois Club, which was forming at UCLA. I accepted and at the first meeting was made education secretary, with duties to educate the members about the life and writings of W.E.B. Dubois. It is possible that many of the other officers and a significant portion of the members also belonged to the Communist Party, however that was not clear to me at the time since members of the CP were generally secretive. One of the few Dubois Club members who openly proclaimed his membership in the CP was Ron Ridenour. In the winter he asked me to join him and another friend, Buddy Bellman, to room together in a house in Venice by the canals. I was happy to leave my crowded quarters on Gayley Street adjoining the UCLA campus and moved in with them. That semester I was mostly submerged in my graduate work, which focused on the fate of the leaders of France's United Front government during World War II.

There was much of interest going on at 412 Carroll Canal. My roommates had an endless group of radical friends who came over to party, sing leftist songs and discuss all kinds of topics. I did get involved in some all-night political discussions with Ridenour and his friends. There was a tremendous intellectual ferment among many college students in that period. Stalin's death ten years earlier, the Cuban Revolution and the split in the International Communist Movement had put many issues out for debate; all topics from the thirties and forties were now being passionately revisited by a new generation of intellectual leftists. The discussions could be heavily contentious. Mao and the Chinese Party were in the process of issuing a series of pamphlets criticizing the lack of revolutionary fervor in most of the official Communist parties around the world, including a just-issued pamphlet calling the Communist Party of the USA to task for selling out the militant struggle in the South and calling particular attention to its lack of involvement in the civil rights movement there.

Much of the history of the thirties was at issue in these discussions and I had some expertise, given my graduate research. We all sat around for endless hours and discussed radical politics from every angle, but in fact did little even to support the civil rights struggle, which was huge in the South and even significant up north in San Francisco. In Los Angeles, the Dubois Club and Friends of SNCC did hold a picket line in front of the Sheraton West Hotel in Beverly Hills to support the struggle against job discrimination at that hotel chain, which had led to many arrests in San Francisco. It was my first picket line and I arrived late and left early; nothing happened in the hour I marched around the hotel with about forty others. Until I arrived in Mississippi it was my only experience in direct action. Not much to speak of.

I can't recall that the Dubois Club made much use of my historical talents to educate them about Dubois or anything else, but they educated me about the ongoing civil rights movement. For me the most significant events were when Student Nonviolent Coordinating Committee (SNCC) members from Mississippi would come to our meetings to speak of the struggle in that state. I was extremely impressed with them; these to me were the real revolutionaries that I had read about, in sharp contrast to the armchair variety that populated the Dubois Club. It was from these speakers from the frontlines in the South that I heard about the upcoming summer project. I had had enough discussions and wanted some experience, so I applied, as did Ron Ridenour, but I was puzzled that none of the other Communist Party members did. It later transpired that the CP nationally was quite suspicious of SNCC and its militant tactics and discouraged its members from joining the project. Ridenour was an undisciplined fellow, who was not in the inner CP circle and felt free to do as he wished. He said, however, that he had permission from the *People's World*, the West Coast Communist Party newspaper, to be their reporter on the project; possibly he just appointed himself.

He, like our driver, became an embarrassment for me later when we got to Ohio. For some reason we left Los Angeles early and the trip dragged out with stops at the Grand Canyon and Petrified Forest in Arizona. While they were interesting places, I just wanted to get where we were going and get out of the crowded car so I could distance myself from those two. The SNCC project had provided us with a reading list to be prepared, and of course, W.E.B. Dubois was part of the list. So I spent much of the trip reading.

William E.B. Dubois was born in a predominantly white town in Massachusetts in 1868; his father was a freed slave and his mother was from a small group of free blacks who owned land in the area. He was soon recognized as a brilliant scholar and attended Harvard, being the first African American ever to earn a PhD there. He then taught as a professor at Atlanta University, a black college in Georgia. His PhD thesis was *The Suppression of the African Slave Trade to the United States,* which I had read as part of my historiography research. In 1909 he became the first black ever to address the American Historical Association. They must not have liked the message since no black was invited again for over three decades.

The slave trade enriched both New England merchants, who shipped the slaves, and the Southern plantation owners, who benefited from the free labor. The West Coast of Africa, which had enjoyed a relatively prosperous feudal-agrarian economy, was devastated for centuries by the slave trade. Even today, from Senegal to Guinea to Ivory Coast, the colonies set up by the American and European slave traders persist as areas of endemic war, ethnic strife and dire poverty. But for the new USA the slave trade was essential to its future prosperity. The vaunted wealth of the United States was not built on a foundation of "freedom and opportunity" but on the wealth produced by the slave trade. The "founding fathers" of this country were well aware of this and Dubois massively documented their obstruction of efforts to end the African slave trade. This only succeeded twenty years into the history of the great democracy and only then because big slave breeder plantations in Virginia and Kentucky found the African slave trade unfair competition.

The slave system as it was practiced in the South from Maryland to Texas was routinely marked by murder, mutilation, rape, torture and forcible removal of children from their parents. Slaves who tried to escape this cruel system, and there were many, could be hunted down or murdered anywhere in the great bastion of freedom, the United States. Slavery was in essence written into the Constitution, a document so revered then and now as a foundation of liberty. Slavery supported an opulent lifestyle for the southern planters, who aped the mores of the English squires. But the southern society was a vicious, violent and depraved social system that also lynched dissidents and robbed millions of poor whites, who had no political rights and often lived on the edge of starvation. The only means for advancement for the poor whites was to become an overseer or guard for the plantation owner.

Both American and English textile manufacturers also became rich off the backs of the slaves (and from the murdered Indians, whose land was cleared for the great plantations). But the rivalry between United States and British textile barons opened up a rift for men and women of good conscience to be able to oppose slavery openly in the United States. Britain had abolished slavery in the West Indies in 1830, and by 1860 the movement to do similarly in the US, or at least to restrict its expansion, threatened the slaveowners so much that they launched an armed rebellion in 1861 with British support.

Dubois documented that it was only the large armies of escaped and freed slaves that allowed the North to finally prevail. When Ulysses S. Grant's armies finally crushed the traitors in 1865 it opened up a social revolution in the South, that had never been seen before in America. This was the subject of Dubois's major work, *Black Reconstruction,* written in 1935. Here Dubois chronicled the great coalition of blacks, northern abolitionists and southern dissidents that formed Republican state governments in the South in the period 1868-1876. Advanced social welfare systems, public education and a vibrant democracy far more advanced than that seen elsewhere in the country marked these Reconstruction governments. In Mississippi the constitutional convention of 1868 led to a particularly radical government. General Adelbert Ames, a Civil War hero from Maine, was governor and later senator of Mississippi. Hiram Revels, the first black ever to enter Congress, also represented the state in the United States Senate. (He too had been a Civil War hero, instrumental in the key Union victory at Vicksburg.) James Alcorn, a white Mississippi dissident, was also originally a key leader in the coalition government. But as the violent reaction led by the Ku Klux Klan mounted in the mid-seventies Alcorn and other white Mississippians fled the coalition. When the Union Army was withdrawn in 1877 the slavocracy retook control of the state.

Our trip to Ohio took us through Arizona and New Mexico where we camped out, but as the three of us got fed up with the cramped car we started to drive straight through the Texas Panhandle, Oklahoma and Missouri. These had been slave territories prior to the Civil War. But the border areas had not been central to the slave plantation economy and were largely pro-Union. However, in the violent aftermath of the Reconstruction they were also centers of the Ku Klux Klan and various criminal racist gangs (like the Jesse James gang) that helped terrorize the South from 1876 to 1954. Segregation had taken complete hold in the Border States that we drove through, but ended there without much violence in the 1954-1960 period, unlike in Mississippi, Alabama and other Deep South states, where no progress was made.

In Mississippi lynchings and murder on a massive scale took place in the last quarter of the nineteenth century as the majority black population in the state was systematically excluded from politics. By the time of the Democratic administration of Woodrow Wilson in 1912, almost all of the black population was disenfranchised and the most stringent Jim Crow laws were enacted. Dubois wrote about this in his masterpiece, *Souls of Black Folk,* written in 1903. This book was required reading by SNCC for all of us prospective volunteers. However, when it first came out and for decades later critics panned it heavily since the prevailing academic wisdom had shifted by 1900. Now the blacks were blamed for a mendacious version of the Reconstruction, which was said to have had destroyed the happy plantation system were it not for the patriotic Ku Klux Klan who put the uppity blacks in their place.

Historians then turned history upside down and Civil War and Reconstruction heroes became villains. My high school history texts pilloried the Reconstruction and praised the Ku Klux Klan. John F. Kennedy's history of the United States Senate, *Profiles in Courage,* was a popular example of the shoddy historical scholarship of the 1950s, which totally bought into the lies and interpretations purveyed by the southern white historians. Dissenting historians like Dubois were marginalized by media and academia, investigated by the FBI, dragged before HUAC (House Un-American Activities Committee), and in Dubois's case eventually hounded out of the country. (This took place during the Kennedy Administration. Kwame Nkrumah welcomed Dubois in Ghana where he died in 1963.) Little wonder that Kennedy himself showed no sympathy at all for the desegregation movement, which gathered steam while he was President.

It was dawn when we crossed the Mississippi River into Illinois. We drove that day through southern Illinois, Indiana and Ohio along the Ohio River, which borders on Kentucky. The economy and culture of the southern part of these northern states was tied to Kentucky, a slave state that nonetheless remained loyal to the Union in the Civil War. But the Jim Crow system took hold in Kentucky too and then percolated north from Kentucky. A revived Ku Klux Klan in the 1920s and 30s established itself as a powerful force in these areas with lynchings of blacks being a weekly occurrence. This was partly in reaction to increased activism of blacks and Communist Party–influenced whites, who together fought Jim Crow.

The Roosevelt Administration had been the first Democratic administration to allow some measure of equality to blacks in its

From 1876 to 1964 every office and facility and even drinking fountains were segregated with obviously inferior facilities for black people. This was the norm in all southern states and even in large parts of the border states, like Maryland and Kentucky.

social programs. This infuriated the Democratic Party's southern white allies and the New Deal backed off of any attempt at reforms in the South. For years in the 1930s attempts to pass a law against lynchings (one would think in the land of liberty and rule of law this would be a slam dunk) were bogged down in the Senate and a law never passed.

Truman desegregated the military and this provoked a revolt by the southern white Democrats, which almost killed his re-election bid in 1948. Kennedy, a prisoner of his own racist interpretation of history, was in addition politically beholden to the southern white Democrats for his razor-thin victory in the election in 1960. He made no moves to even uphold the rule of law in the South, never mind to oppose desegregation actively. By the time he was assassinated in 1963 there were fewer blacks registered to vote in Mississippi than in 1900; every school and public institution in the state was totally segregated, even down to the drinking fountains at the courthouses. The Mississippi Democratic Party completely excluded blacks, and the same system of violent intimidation and depraved morality in officialdom that reigned a hundred years prior under slavery held sway with little visible change.

Into this fascist system a courageous band of black SNCC workers had been struggling for three years, trying without success to register black people to vote.[2] Jailed, beaten and killed for their efforts, they were ignored by the media and federal government. Now this was about to change: with the full glare of major media publicity a thousand mostly northern college students would enter the fray to share weal and woe with the black people of Mississippi.

---

2. The Student Nonviolent Coordinating Committee, as the name implies, was set up in the wake of the 1960-61 sit-in movement to coordinate the sit-ins. The black colleges mostly in North Carolina and Tennessee, where the repression was not as severe as in the Deep South, provided most of the initial chapters. Soon Howard University in Washington, DC became the largest chapter as its members fought to integrate facilities in the nation's capital and the surrounding suburbs of Maryland. Many of the SNCC chapter leaders went to the Deep South by 1964 to work on voter registration.

The segregation laws were called Jim Crow Laws. ("Jim Crow" was another insulting term applied by whites to black men in the nineteenth century.) These highly detailed laws made any integrated facilities illegal and subjected the owners to severe criminal penalties if violated. Where segregated facilities were impractical, such as libraries, beaches, swimming pools, or amusement parks blacks were simply banned. Jim Crow Laws also required segregated housing, outlawed interracial marriage or even social mingling, forced blacks to sit in the back of the bus or train, and included a myriad of other regulations, some quite arcane. In this picture volunteer, Karen Koonan, rallies Freedom School students.

We entered the town of Oxford, Ohio, and found our way to the Western College for Women, which had donated its campus to the National Council of Churches, after a Kentucky college backed out under pressure. The National Council of Churches was the official sponsor of the training for the student volunteers, but in fact SNCC ran every aspect of the training. We were two days early, since we drove straight through, but the SNCC people found us housing that night; somehow the donated clothes were taken to the right people, and we settled in. It was June 12, 1964.

UHURU means Freedom in Swahili.

2

The Training in Oxford, Ohio

How beauteous mankind is! Oh brave new world
That has such people in it!

The Tempest

There was probably a policy of not rooming people from the same area together since we three were all housed in separate rooms with new roommates still to arrive. So I saw little of my car mates that week. The driver left sometime in the middle of training without a word of goodbye. As for Ridenour, I would see him sitting ostentatiously in the grassy plaza typing away at what I assumed to be stories for the *People's World*. He was quite a curiosity dressed in fatigues with an army cap, purposely looking the part of a Cuban Fidelista. I gave him a wide berth, not wanting anyone to know that I was associated with him. At one time in the middle of the week he came to me and said that Jim Forman wanted to kick him out, but that John Lewis had intervened and they would send him to Pascagoula on the coast, where they thought he could do little harm. (In the end John Lewis was wrong, and he caused so much antagonism and dissension among the staff that the project expelled him altogether before a month was up.) I was soon to make new friends with the roommates assigned to me.

It was easy to tell the SNCC veterans from the volunteers, who were arriving slowly that day and the next. The SNCC workers were with few exceptions dressed in white t-shirts and denim overalls. They were almost all black, mostly men but some women, and, although my age or younger, they carried themselves with such maturity and such an air of confidence, that, upon sight, they commanded tremendous respect. To talk with them only reinforced this first impression. They had been through a lot, had seen best friends killed and maimed; they themselves had all spent time in Mississippi jails and had been beaten there and come close to death more than a few times. To me, a man who had read stories of the Resistance in World War II and of revolutionaries in Cuba and elsewhere, it was indeed a brave new world. I considered myself lucky and honored to be working under such people.

I went to a main hall where they were having a meeting. There were maybe eighty people there, mostly SNCC workers. The meeting was led by Bob Moses. I kept quiet and stayed in the back of the room, but nobody objected to my presence and several other early arrived volunteers came too. Some spoke. Moses quietly called on whoever raised their hand and everyone had their say. People spoke their hearts out, but without debating or often even referring to previous speakers. The subject was, even at this late date, whether to go ahead with the project. People spoke of the armed preparations the state was making and of the threats bandied about from officials and others to kill all the volunteers and SNCC workers. Some voiced distrust that the white volunteers could cope under these circumstances; others felt the project was too provocative and the consequences might be unimaginable. I found myself wondering if we would be sent home, yet people were really just venting. Bob Moses understood this and let everyone have their say and voiced sympathy to their concerns. The discussion went on into the early hours of the morning and then just broke up as people got tired and went to bed. There was no conclusion or resolution; the SNCC people, if not the volunteers, understood, however, that they were committed and the project would go on. The next evening there was another meeting, but by this time dozens of volunteers had arrived and wanted to sit in on the meeting; we were then told that the meeting was closed to non-SNCC members and the training would begin the next morning.

The discussion I witnessed was the continuation of a discussion of many meetings and many months. In November 1963 eighty white students had come down from Stanford and Yale to support the Freedom Ballot; their presence and the media attention it generated seemed to restrain the deputies and police from their usual unbridled violence. That experience led to a proposal at the Greenville SNCC meeting of mid-November for a summer project. A long and intense discussion followed with no resolution.

The arguments for the project revolved around the strategic need to break the Mississippi system of violent intimidation by forcing the people and government of the USA, the self-appointed leader of the "free world," to see what kind of state-sponsored terrorism was going on in their own country against US citizens who only wanted to register to vote. Bringing in large numbers of white students from elite campuses would guarantee media attention. The arguments against the project were mostly tactical: such a project would only incense white Mississippians and increase violence, and Mississippi blacks would bear the brunt of it; highly educated white students would tend to take over and the carefully built local structures would be endangered; white students could not blend into the community and would be in greater danger than the black SNCC veterans. The events were to show that both sides of the debate were correct. The tactical dangers pointed to by the opponents all came to pass one way or the other and caused serious problems and some tragic losses. But in the end it was due to the visionaries like Bob Moses, Fannie Lou Hamer and Lawrence Guyot, who had argued for doing something "big," that a big strategic victory was won.

More meetings were needed to bring the SNCC staff together around so contentious an issue, and a December 1963 meeting agreed to a small summer project of no more than one hundred volunteers. That same month an SNCC executive committee passed a resolution for a project with "as many people as necessary." In January 1964 a Freedom Day with 150 white clergymen as witnesses showed that it was possible to restrain the police and 150 blacks were able to register to vote. A COFO (SNCC and allies) meeting after that event again discussed the summer project. During the meeting another civil rights worker, Louis Allen, was reported murdered. Bob Moses said they had to do something big or the best among them would be killed one by one. The majority agreed and the project was organized, but as I saw that June the misgivings did not go away, nor should they have for they were very, very real.

The state's governor, senators and others all denounced the project as an "invasion," which must be met very forcefully. The capital city of Jackson purchased an advanced armored car to break up demonstrations and readied vast barbed-wire enclosures for a Mississippi concentration camp; the highway patrol was re-armed and jails made ready everywhere. At the state level much of this was for show so that the yokels would see their politicians as action oriented. The danger was more at the local level, where ignorant sheriffs and police tried to match these state preparations, but the locals were much more in earnest; in many counties sheriffs deputized Ku Klux Klan members and other local thugs; the gun stores did a booming business, dynamite was stockpiled, as arms and wild rumors about the communist invasion were passed around in equal measure. The local FBI were in cahoots with the sheriffs and the national FBI director loudly announced he was not going to wet-nurse "troublemakers," purposely giving a free pass to any violence state and local officials wished to visit upon the invaders. At the state level and in some counties the violent rhetoric was furious, but the actual plans in most counties called for no more than strong police measures against the volunteers and SNCC, extremely harsh economic penalties against any prospective black voters and

"Oxford orientation - 1964." Drawing by Tracy Sugarman

A strategy session for voter registration volunteers, in Ruleville. John Harris is on the right and Jim Dann (author) is in the center.

a large measure of intimidation by nightriders. These were the counties ruled by the White Citizen Councils (WCC), ideologically very much akin to our modern Tea Party types.

But in some counties, especially the most impoverished rural ones with rolling hills— counties like Amite, Talahatchie and Neshoba—the sheriffs were barely literate, ignorant brutes who took the violent rhetoric from the state level quite seriously. These were the Ku Klux Klan–controlled counties, and here the actual plans were to deal no less than death to the invaders. Lynchings and murder were in the blood of these sheriffs and deputies and the encouragement from the highest state officials and even the FBI director in Washington (at that time the infamous J. Edgar Hoover) seemed to guarantee them safety from any justice.

Just before the training began a black delegation from Mississippi, including the widow of murdered Louis Allen, went to Washington to beg for some kind of federal signal that they would protect voter registration. President Lyndon Johnson was out of town, Attorney General Robert F. Kennedy was unavailable, Congress would not hold hearings and the FBI rebuffed the delegation as subversives and communist dupes. At the training we were addressed by Assistant Attorney General John Doar, the most sympathetic Federal Justice Department official. He told us that there could be no federal protection and we would have to take our chances in a hostile state as blacks had done for generations. Doar was no doubt uncomfortable with the position of Kennedy and Johnson, but his hands were tied. Johnson was worried about his re-election in the fall and feared losing the support of the white Southern states. Bob Moses, seeing the incredulous and hostile reaction of the volunteers, told us that Doar was just being honest. We were, of course, free to go home, as the driver of our car from Los Angeles had done already. A few others left during the training; some parents fetched others still who were under twenty-one, but the vast majority of students stayed, though now with fewer illusions. I, myself, trusted the veteran SNCC workers to keep me safe far more than the FBI or any prospective federal marshals. I was also already somewhat fatalistic in those days and was ready to take my chances. While I was scared at times, I never considered going home. I felt that I had made a commitment and would stick with it.

Non-violent training was a major feature of the week. We had daily sessions teaching us positions to minimize bodily damage during a police beating. There was role-playing with some, often black, SNCC veterans playing the role of sheriffs and deputies and we playing the role of hapless demonstrators taking insults and beatings. These sessions were the most difficult for me, since I was not inclined to passively let myself get beaten or adopt the fetal position, which was taught us. But I did recognize that in some situations this was by far the best approach. In the year that followed I never had occasion to use the non-violent training. I took both my beatings standing up. One was by the police and I did not resist, the other was by a local racist and I handed him back a few blows of my own.

There were 250 to 300 volunteers at our training session that began June 13. About ninety percent were white, the rest black. The SNCC staff numbered about a hundred and they were about ninety percent black. In our session, which was devoted to those doing voter registration work, about seventy-five percent of the volunteers were male. I would say that roughly the same male-female percentage applied to the SNCC staff. The second session for Freedom School teachers, given the following week, numbered close to four hundred and was probably seventy-five percent female with even fewer black volunteers. The Freedom School session began a week after we left for Mississippi. In the course of the summer possibly another two or three hundred came down; they were given a weekend of training in SNCC headquarters in Jackson. While I had had contact with radical, socialist and even communist students at UCLA and had a very slight experience in participating in some civil rights pickets in Los Angeles, the majority of students did not come from a left-wing background and many had no prior experience with any kind of civil rights work. On the other hand, some black students like John Harris had been heavily involved in civil rights in the North, had a vast experience in sit-ins and civil disobedience and had faced down cops in many confrontations. More than a few white students, like Andrew Goodman, also had a much more significant civil rights experience than I. Subsequent surveys found that a significant number of volunteers had parents who had at one time been active in radical and socialist movements. On the other hand, many were just people of good will incensed by the injustice of the South and who wanted to do the right thing. I was in many ways in the middle in both experience and in exposure to radical politics. In all the group of volunteers was quite a mixture and presented a formidable challenge to the SNCC veterans, who had to bring this disparate group together and design training that would work for everyone there.

Half of the students came from the elite universities, such as Stanford, University of California, Ivy League and University of Chicago. Of the SNCC staff there were many who had not gone to college at all, although the top leaders like Moses and Lewis were highly educated. Obviously there was a cultural chasm between the leaders of the training and the volunteers, but by and large the volunteers were very good at accepting their subordinate role. Deep suspicions were bridged as well as could be hoped for in the week, and bonds began to develop. I was very conscious of this problem and always felt that it was I who needed to prove myself to the SNCC staff. I had no problem following their leadership since in my life I had not yet met people whom I respected more.

The training was held under the auspices of the National Council of Churches (NCC), an organization that ostensibly represented thirty-one religions and forty million members. But in reality their civil rights arm was only involved and most of the church leaders either stayed aloof or were hostile to the project. The Southern White Baptists, one of their biggest denominations, quit the National Council over the project. But the NCC funding of the training was very helpful and gave important political cover for SNCC, given the hostility of the Johnson Administration. The NCC also sent down some three hundred ministers, rabbis, priests and seminary students to help with our spiritual needs. The hope that the National Council of Churches would make contact and build bridges with the white churches was not realized, with very few exceptions. The white churches of Mississippi were racist to the core and indeed gave biblical backup to the notions of black inferiority and the need to firmly resist integration. White Baptist preachers were in some cases leaders of the Ku Klux Klan and helped burn down black Baptist churches.

The Council of Federated Organizations (COFO) was the leadership organization for the project. It was made up of the Student Nonviolent Coordinating Committee (SNCC), the Congress of Racial Equality (CORE), the Southern Christian Leadership Conference (SCLC) and the National Association for the Advancement of Colored People (NAACP). In reality, however, SNCC provided about one hundred staff and CORE possibly as many as thirty to forty, while less than half a dozen came from the NAACP and SCLC. The SCLC, led by Martin Luther King, was involved in a parallel struggle in parts of Alabama, had few young members and could not spare any resources for Mississippi. The national NAACP was quite cool to the project, since they were, of the major civil rights organizations, the most closely tied to Johnson's re-election efforts. However, their Mississippi members were largely supportive. The NAACP was the oldest civil rights organization, founded by W.E.B. Dubois in 1903. After the Supreme Court desegregation case in 1954, which the NAACP had litigated, won and with great difficulty followed up state by state (with no support at all from the federal Justice Department), the organization rapidly built up chapters in Mississippi. A few of these brave men and women registered to vote in the aftermath of 1954. Then the state enacted laws to prevent any further black voters from registering, and county sheriffs followed up with violence and intimidation.

Medgar Evers headed the NAACP staff in the state before 1963, but Byron De La Beckwith, a White Citizens' Council member shot him in the back in June 1963 and then bragged openly of the murder. De La Beckwith was arrested but acquitted after the Mississippi governor, Ross Barnet, visited him in jail with much fanfare to show state support for the murder of civil rights leaders. The funeral march for Evers on June 15, 1963, attended by 5,000, was brutally attacked by the Jackson police. After that the national NAACP, working in tandem with the Kennedy Administration, decided to avoid any further confrontation in that city. The young NAACP activists in Jackson then largely left Jackson for the rural counties and turned to SNCC, which had stepped into the breach. The SNCC workers became the heart and soul of the movement in Mississippi. But many older NAACP leaders in the various counties provided crucial support and were to become local leaders of the movements that were eventually built up. We were to find that in Sunflower County the older NAACP members would often be the rock-solid base of support that we needed when we entered a town. CORE was mainly a Northern civil rights organization; the CORE workers that went to the state were content to accept SNCC leadership. For political purposes SNCC put CORE in charge of the area around Meridian, MS, and the second in command of COFO, Dave Dennis, was a CORE member. (Jackson, the state capital, was assigned to the NAACP, but very little happened there that summer.) Thus, in reality, COFO was virtually indistinguishable from SNCC.

COFO was an initiative of Bob Moses and some local leaders from CORE and the NAACP. It was initially funded by the Voter Education Project (VEP), which had been set up by allies of the Kennedy Administration in 1961. John Kennedy, the self-professed leader of the "free world," had been profoundly embarrassed by the violent state-sponsored terrorism in the South against desegregation efforts in 1958-1961 and the virtual outlawing of the NAACP in many Southern states. The idea was to turn the student activists away from direct action against desegregation to voter registration. But when those leading the voter registration campaign in Mississippi, Alabama, South Carolina, Georgia and Louisiana were subjected to police brutality for their efforts, and when blacks who dared to register were subjected to extreme economic reprisals, and little progress could be seen in the numbers, the idea of voter registration no longer seemed like such a good idea in Washington. In Mississippi the many murders of leaders of the voter registration effort were additionally a great embarrassment to Kennedy. The assassins were all known to the police and FBI, and some were state and county officials themselves. Rather than enforce the law in the South, Kennedy chose to end the confrontation by discouraging any further voter registration efforts in the Deep South. In mid-1963 Voter Education Project funds were cynically cut off to the Council of Federated Organizations (COFO) and diverted to states where the resistance to black voting was not significant. This caused a financial crisis for COFO, but it was not too serious since SNCC workers were used to making do with very little and the black people of Mississippi were generous and more than willing to share food and shelter with the SNCC workers.

The training concentrated on teaching us how to register voters. The Mississippi voter application had twenty-one questions, including reading and interpreting arcane sections of the state constitution. So educating people to be able to fill out the application was part of the process. But it was not the key aspect since the white registrar of each county was the sole judge of the interpretation and the deal was fixed to begin with. Black college graduates were almost always flunked while completely illiterate whites were usually passed. (Numerous witnesses in a subsequent federal court case demonstrated this.) Getting blacks to go to the county courthouse was seen as the key aspect, since SNCC knew that only a mass movement would change the dynamic. But going to the county courthouse was an act of great courage for blacks since economic reprisals were absolutely certain and violent retribution not at all unlikely. And all this just to demonstrate a desire to register to vote, while it was known full well the black applications would be inexorably denied by the registrars.

Approaching rural black people in a way that respected them, understanding their hesitations and sympathizing with what they had had to put up with their whole lives was not an easy lesson for white students from the best colleges in the North to learn. Yet on the whole we passed the test. The SNCC veterans were helpful teachers and the volunteers really wanted to do the right thing. Role-playing was the main method of instruction.

Late one afternoon in the training I took the part of a young volunteer trying to get a black farmer to register to vote. Jim

Forman played the part of the farmer, "Mr. Davis"; I was accompanied by an SNCC worker and another volunteer. The SNCC worker introduced me to Forman. I stepped forward and extended my hand, "I am very happy to meet you, Mr. Davis." Jim Forman acted out the part and very tentatively took my hand. This kind of respectful greeting from a white to a black in Mississippi was completely unknown at the time and was essential and in itself a powerful political statement. "Mr. Davis, we hope that you and your two sons will go to the courthouse in Clarksdale this Saturday. We are all going to drive down together in the morning. I know you understand how important it is for you all to register to vote this summer," I continued. Forman was polite and attentive, but he made it clear that he was not going to do it. "We'll have to see, Mr. Dann. Voting's never been our concern. We have all we can do… My boys are good boys. But they have a lot to do right here on the place." The interplay was realistic and the rejection was to be far more common than not, especially with blacks who had a lot to lose economically. Yet the act of asking respectfully and of a white person understanding and abiding by a decision by a black man was perhaps the most important thing. I, to some extent, dimly understood this at the time. But both Forman and Charles McLaurin, the SNCC leader in Sunflower County, who observed the interplay, understood the significance much more.[1] They must have agreed afterwards that I would go to Sunflower County and work under McLaurin.

The next morning Jim Forman informed me that I was to be part of the Ruleville (Sunflower County) project. The SNCC people were very much aware that major media attention would save lives. They also understood that concentrating the media on one project would be the best strategy to keep attention on the front pages. Ruleville was to be the flagship project in that regard. The first reason had to do with the SNCC leader there, McLaurin, who was in my view the

---

1. Account taken from *Stranger at the Gates* by Tracy Sugarman, p. 31. I recall the incident but don't remember the exact words.

Charles McLaurin, leader of the Sunflower County Project. He modestly called himself a "foot soldier" in the Civil Rights struggle. But in fact he was much more than that, while not one of the famous "generals" who made the news, he was a singularly effective and intelligent leader, loyal to his "troops," but able to make use of everyone's talents in the struggle.

most mature, intelligent and dedicated SNCC field worker in the Delta. He could hold a project together, if anyone could. The second reason was that Ruleville was home to the most dynamic and articulate of all the local leaders in the state, Fannie Lou Hamer. She was already famous in the media for her heart-wrenching story of the police beating she was subjected to in Winona, which left her lame in one leg. To reinforce them Forman carefully picked the people for the Ruleville project. Len Edwards—the son of Don Edwards, a congressman from California—would be a media draw and would also go. John Harris, who was the president of the largest SNCC chapter in the country at Howard University would also go to Ruleville. Dale Gronemeir, a national secretary for the Committee to Abolish the House Un-American Activities Committee (HUAC) would head up communications and handle the media. The others were picked based on their performance at the role-playing sessions. Forman was impressed with the way I had handled myself so I was chosen to go, as were a dozen others.

Gronemeir proved to be an excellent press secretary and he had his hands full that summer. The three most-read magazines of that era were: *Life, Look* and *Saturday Evening Post.* The latter two agreed to have reporters embedded with the project for the first few weeks, and *Life,* as well as CBS and NBC, had reporters who would concentrate on Ruleville. Len Edwards and Fannie Lou Hamer were almost regular features on the evening news, while the rest of us also managed to get our pictures in the major magazines of the day. So the careful planning for the project included a major push for media attention. Unknown to me in Ohio I was chosen to be part of that push. At the time I was honored and happy to have done well enough to get a spot in any project. I didn't know Mrs. Hamer or Charles McLaurin.

"Fannie Lou with volunteers - 1964" by Tracy Sugarman

Fannie Lou Hamer at the Freedom School in Ruleville probably during an adult literacy class. These classes were among the most effective and important contributions of the Freedom School teachers.

Shortly after I had committed myself to Ruleville, James Chaney, a bright young man of twenty-one and one of the CORE staff members in Meridian, came to my room. He too had seen the interplay with Forman and was looking for volunteers for his project. He asked me if I would go to Meridian with him. I said I would be happy to but I had already promised that I would go to Ruleville. He then turned to one of my roommates, Andrew Goodman, and asked him. Goodman agreed and committed himself to the Meridian project. Goodman and I had had several friendly interchanges, and for a day or two of the training we sort of hung out together. Goodman came from a progressive Jewish family in New York; he had been active in CORE in New York, where he had been attending Queens College. His parents were totally supportive of his participation in the project. We liked each other, and I was a bit disappointed and a bit envious when he told me before the end of the training that he had to leave early with Chaney; there was some kind of emergency and the CORE leader at Meridian, Michael Schwerner, decided that the three of them should skip the final two days of training and return to Meridian. Unknown to them the chief investigator for the Mississippi State Sovereignty Commission got their car description and license plate and gave it to the sheriff of Neshoba County, near Meridian, who immediately laid plans for the lynching of the three.

A black church had been burned down and early in the morning of June 20, while we were still in the final day of training, the three went to investigate and meet with the members of the congregation, who had been supporting voter registration efforts. The three were arrested according to plan by Deputy Sheriff Cecil Price, a Ku Klux Klan member, and held incommunicado in jail until dark. Then they were released and followed by Deputy Sherriff Price who stopped them again. This time Price held them in a remote road until the rest of the murderers arrived. Some dozen or more of the local Klan arrived, headed by a preacher named Killen and Sheriff Rainey. (The number of actual murderers at the scene was never

Left to right: Andrew Goodman, James Chaney, and Michael Schwerner. This FBI poster was put up before the bodies were discovered. The FBI subsequently liked to take credit for cracking the case, but in fact their publicists were much more effective than their investigators. The FBI investigation was marked by amateurish bungling, monumental incompetence, and a blindness induced by both an unprofessional and cozy relationship with the local law enforcement, some of whom were the killers, as well as an obsession with the left-wing views of the victims.

definitively determined, but there were probably about two dozen, and other local, county and state police were directly or indirectly involved in some aspects of the lynching.) They brutally beat Chaney, breaking many of his bones, and then shot him. They also shot Schwerner and Goodman to death and buried all three in an earthen dam. As the rest of us in Ohio were boarding the buses eighteen hours later rumors that three workers were missing were already circulating, but I didn't know who they were or where they were from.

Some volunteers left the project on the basis of these rumors as the serious dangers we would face now became much more than hypothetical. Some had been leaving throughout the training; some under twenty-one were gathered up by parents, who also became privy to the knowledge of the dangerous ground we were about to tread. Throughout the training Bob Moses encouraged the volunteers who had not realized the dangers of the situation or who had trouble handling it to go home. He repeatedly emphasized that there was no shame in that and that they could be useful in the North as support to the summer project. None of us could be in any way unaware of what we were facing or going down there with false illusions.

The SNCC veterans were generally modest and did not pretend to have all the answers. The training often amounted to no more than letting people talk and ask questions. Nobody had any pretenses or traded on their experience to lord it over the volunteers. Everybody, veterans and volunteers alike, had a sincere interest in making the project work. That attitude among all was the essence of the training. I had never seen anything like that atmosphere in my life, and never was to see it again after I left Mississippi.

Earlier in the training a crisis had arisen that severely tested the cohesion of the project. Moses had been telling the assembled volunteers that they were not to go to Mississippi to save the "Mississippi Negro" but because our freedom and theirs were linked. Did we understand this? Many as it turned out did not. A film was then shown to us, which featured people saying why they wanted to vote. A scene followed, which featured the white registrar of voters for Tallahatchie County; he had a huge potbelly and a tiny, stupid-looking head. This stereotype of the racist Southerner was just that. Physical type did not necessarily indicate anything; we were to be attacked that summer by fat and slim, short and tall, ugly and relatively handsome. But in this case many of the volunteers found him ridiculous and laughed. I didn't laugh, but could see, given the tension of the last few days, why many volunteers did. The SNCC workers in the room said "Shush." What they understood was that these people were brutes and killers. Many SNCC workers had been brutally beaten by precisely this sociological type. Tallahatchie County had been the scene just eight years earlier of the brutal lynching of Emmett Till;[2] perhaps this registrar was among the killers; if not he was undoubtedly friends with the murderers. The volunteers, who laughed, perhaps, were anticipating villains that looked like they came out of a James Bond movie and were amused and maybe relieved to see that something that looked so indolent and stupid would be the opposition. But the SNCC veterans knew better. Actions, not looks, defined the racist enemy. In fact Sheriff Rainey and some of his gang had the same physical look as this registrar, but the preacher who was the Klan leader of the lynching was slim and tall, others of the gang were short and sallow, and Deputy Sherriff Price might from his pictures be considered a good-looking man, but each one and together were all ruthless and merciless killers.

The movie went on as a black man who had tried to register to vote told about the night two young girls in his house were shot by nightriders while they were watching television. His wife came on and continued the story. She was, to be sure, dressed poorly and not to the tastes of Northern University students. Some of the students started laughing again. That I found incomprehensible given the pathos of what was being said. But I suppose to be fair many volunteers had found the training wrenching and scary and desperately needed some kind of comic relief. But the SNCC veterans were incensed at the reaction and for many it seemed proof of their long-held misgivings about the viability of this type of project. Some walked out. But others turned on the lights and turned the episode into a teachable moment. A long, heartfelt discussion followed as the volunteers faced up to their own prejudices. It lasted several hours. I said very little, but listened a lot. I remember being particularly impressed with the passionate way a young woman from Cincinnati, named Liz Fusco, confronted her own past racist ideas and was determined to learn and be transformed. She was about my age, three or four years older than the average volunteer.

---

2. Emmett Till was a fourteen-year-old boy from Chicago who, while visiting relatives in Mississippi, was murdered after reportedly whistling at a white woman.

She was subsequently asked to become head of the Freedom Schools in our project in Sunflower County.

The discussion kind of petered out in the evening, with as usual nothing definitively settled but everyone the wiser. For us volunteers, the lesson of the necessity to banish Northern university modes of thinking, to be respectful of the people we came to serve and to carefully listen to the blacks of Mississippi would help to get us through the summer. But the lesson would have to be constantly reinforced by the local leaders and SNCC veterans. Where we had strong and assertive local leaders as in Ruleville the project had great prospects of being very successful. Additionally I think the long discussion convinced even the SNCC veterans of at least the sincerity and seriousness of the volunteers. At the end we all held hands and sang "We Shall Overcome."

The singing of the same anthem and many other freedom songs went steadily; it seemed it was a good hour before we boarded the buses, singing particularly passionately on that last afternoon for the overnight ride to Mississippi. This time a then-popular song, "We May Never See Each Other Again," was added to the list for the first time. Almost everyone had tears in their eyes, even some of the SNCC veterans. The mystery of the missing workers in Meridian was being whispered about and everyone expected that indeed some of us would not survive the summer. Our particular bus included both the Ruleville and Clarksdale projects, maybe forty of us altogether. We slept through Kentucky and Tennessee, but dawn was breaking as we crossed the border into Mississippi and we all looked nervously to the rear of the bus for nightriders or police. But the road was empty, and in Clarksdale we said goodbye to our comrades going to work there. Ruleville was less than an hour away and the sun was high in the sky when we drove in to the dusty dirt roads of the black area of town. The bus driver was visibly relieved at having discharged his passengers and couldn't wait to leave.

Everyone's fear and nervousness evaporated under the warm and sunny greeting we received from Fannie Lou Hamer. We had stopped in front of her house, and she came bounding out of the house nearly shouting her greetings before we could collect our luggage from the bus driver, who was as eager to leave as Hamer was to have us here. She had long championed this project and argued for it at every SNCC and COFO meeting. Not till we arrived was she sure it would come to fruition. Len Edwards would stay at her house, guaranteeing media attention on her. Charles McLaurin efficiently assigned housing for the rest of us elsewhere in the black community of one thousand or so.

Local students walked us to our hosts' homes. Mine was two or three blocks away from Hamer's. I don't recall the name of my host; she was a single woman of about forty or fifty. She greeted me warmly. The house was a simple wood structure, very clean and with a neat garden. She showed me how to do my laundry in a basin with a scrub-board, a new experience for me. Dinner served in the afternoon was beans and cornbread; it was delicious and I was hungry. In the evening we went to the local church, which was next to Fannie Lou Hamer's house. There would be a mass meeting for the blacks of Ruleville; she and McLaurin wanted to introduce us to the community. It was June 21, 1964.

STATE OF MISSISSIPPI
Some of the Main Freedom Summer Projects in 1964

SUNFLOWER COUNTY, MISSISSIPPI

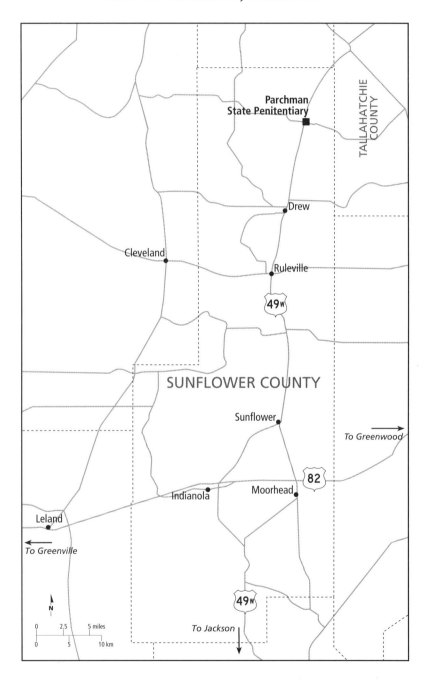

Parchman
State Penitentiary

TALLAHATCHIE
COUNTY

Drew

Cleveland

Ruleville

49ᵂ

SUNFLOWER COUNTY

Sunflower

To Greenwood

82

Indianola

Moorhead

Leland

To Greenville

49ᵂ

To Jackson

N

0   2.5   5 miles
0   5   10 km

3

Our Base in Ruleville

....

Cowards die many times before their deaths;
The valiant never taste of death but once.

Julius CAESAR

The lynching of James Chaney, Michael Schwerner and Andrew Goodman had a profound effect on the summer project, and I personally never forgot them. We can be assured that Chaney, Schwerner and Goodman showed the bravery in their last moments that had marked all their lives. As a high school student Chaney had showed great courage in wearing a NAACP button to school; he was expelled at once. Schwerner had faced death more than once in the year he was in Meridian. I personally knew Goodman to be a young man of justice and courage. As for the cowardly brutes who perpetrated the deed, we know little. They never showed remorse or confessed in any serious way. So we don't know for sure the grisly details of the lynching, which of them were actually present or how many others in Mississippi law enforcement were privy to the plot. We do know that the leader of the gang was a preacher, that most participants were small businessmen and that local, county and state law enforcement were all involved in some fashion. The FBI had fifteen agents in the state at the time, and while they had a cozy relationship to local law enforcement, they also had a "Don't ask, don't tell" policy when it came to lynchings. So they probably were not privy to the plot, but we can't be certain. But certainly the FBI knew who the likely lynchers were in a given area and strong words of warning a priori could have prevented the deed.

When the national press raised more and more serious questions as the days passed the state governor, Paul Johnson, opined that the missing civil rights workers were in Cuba. The arch-segregationist senator, James Eastland, who owned a plantation in Sunflower County, declared to his fellow senators in the US Senate that the trio was in Harlem having a drunken party. (To even make these statements the governor and senator must have been told by someone in on the plot that the bodies were buried in a place where nobody would find them.) In Washington J. Edgar Hoover, the head of the FBI, defiantly refused to investigate and took the opportunity to once again assure Mississippi law enforcement that he would not protect these troublemakers.

This was the situation a few days after we had arrived in Ruleville on June 25 when Stokely Carmichael and three other SNCC workers drove into town. Carmichael was district director and leader of the Leflore County project adjacent to Sunflower County and carried a message from Bob Moses, who was by now certain that the three were dead. Moses issued orders that all volunteers and SNCC workers were to remain in place and not to venture out even to register voters at the courthouse. With Carmichael's group came also a rumor that now three more civil rights workers were missing in Humphreys County. I did a quick calculation and remarked to a fellow volunteer that at that rate fewer than half of us would be alive at the end of the summer. As it turned out the missing Humphreys County volunteers had been arrested, but they were soon released safely.

We were indeed then confined to Ruleville, where we canvassed the black neighborhood and helped set up the Freedom School. But for a week there wasn't that much canvassing to do if you couldn't go to the courthouse. Soon the Freedom School teachers arrived, which left us voter registration types feeling a little useless. We all kept our eyes glued to the TV news at night. (In those days 24-hour TV news was unknown; local Mississippi radio would not touch the story of the missing trio, so we had to wait for the nightly network news.)

President Johnson was now faced with a dilemma. He had based his re-election strategy on carrying the South. But now the national outcry was so great that he risked losing New York and California. That was a poor political trade-off. When Johnson decided to act he could be decisive and ruthless and he now lost patience. First, Hoover was called in and told to find those bodies or lose his job; other political reprisals were also probably threatened against him. Second, he sent in one hundred and fifty northern FBI agents to oversee their Mississippi counterparts. Third, he ordered the Navy based in Mississippi to send sailors to Neshoba County to look for the workers. Naval divers then searched every swamp and bayou in the county. Fourth, he muscled through Congress the Civil Rights Act of 1964, which banned segregation even in private businesses.

Although the Navy didn't find the missing trio, what they found was shocking enough. They found bodies of eight black men probably previously murdered by Rainey and his cronies in the Klan, although this was never proved nor even investigated. Three of them were black civil rights workers; the other five were never identified. Forty days later, using what today would be called enhanced interrogation techniques, contractors for the FBI finally forced a highway patrolman to reveal where the bodies were buried and name the other killers. The state and the FBI refused to let an independent autopsy be done and just said the three were shot. The families had to go to court to eventually get an autopsy, which revealed that James Chaney had been brutally tortured before being shot. The evidence was turned over to the state, which refused to prosecute the killers for murder. That winter the FBI, under intense pressure from Johnson, did arrest nineteen of the conspirators and charge them with federal crimes. But the white juries only convicted seven, including Price; Rainey was acquitted and finished his term as sheriff. (The subsequently elected sheriff of the county was another of the arrested but acquitted killers.) None of the convicted felons served more than six years for the murders. Not until 2005 did the state finally prosecute the case and then only against Roy Killen, the leader of the gang, who was sentenced to sixty years.

The night we arrived in Ruleville we gathered at the Williams Chapel Missionary Baptist church. The black residents of Ruleville were already streaming in, unafraid of the mayor, one Mr. Dorrough, and other racist thugs driving by in their pickups with rifles and shotguns prominently displayed. We initially were seated in the pews with the older residents. Young teenage girls took up the front rows; these were the heart of the student activists from Ruleville. (The youth population was mostly female; young men emigrated to Chicago as quickly as they could in search of jobs and freedom.) Charles McLaurin stood in front and asked that we volunteers come forward and introduce ourselves, saying where we were from. I said, "Jim Dann from UCLA in Los Angeles"; the others said similar things. Except for "John Harris, Howard University in Washington," we were all white; there were two young women and about ten young men. The audience was thunderous in its applause and very warm in its welcoming. Charles led us in singing various freedom songs; most of them were old gospel songs, with the lyrics a little updated for the civil rights movement. Others with their references to the Jews in captivity in Egypt were quite clear as to which contemporary people in captivity were being referenced. Fannie Lou Hamer would often change the lyrics to be more explicit: "the people Moses led" became "the people Bob Moses led"; "children of the Israelites" became " the people fighting for their rights"; "the hypocrites turning back" became "the Uncle Toms turning back." That night the singing was so loud and

"Charles McLaurin, SNCC, at Williams Chapel, Ruleville, MS. 1964" by Tracy Sugarman

Charles McLaurin speaks to a mass meeting at the Williams Chapel, introducing the new volunteers. Deeply imbedded with the community, he was loved, protected, and respected. The volunteers never would have been accepted without him.

exuberant that it shook the wooden walls and could be heard on the highway at the gas station, where the racists and their pickups gathered.

The small wooden chapel had been used for civil rights meetings since August 1962, at the initiative of Joe and Rebecca McDonald, leaders of the church and friends of the NAACP leader Amzie Moore from the nearby town of Cleveland. The mayor of Ruleville, Charles Dorrough, revoked the church's tax exemptions and water use, but to no effect.

At one of the earliest meetings James Bevel, Bob Moses and some SNCC workers then based in Cleveland met Fannie Lou Hamer, a leader of the church and then the timekeeper in the nearby Marlow plantation. She then joined them and eighteen others in a rented bus to Indianola, the county seat, to attempt to register to vote. To fight the fear on the way down and the disappointment on the way back she used her powerful singing voice to keep the bus rolling in song. Moses was equally impressed and asked McLaurin to leave Cleveland and move to Ruleville to join forces with Hamer. Marlow, the plantation owner, had the opposite reaction; he told Hamer to rescind her application. She told him that she was registering for herself not for him; he then fired her on the spot and evicted her and her family from the house they rented on the plantation. She then moved into a friend's house in Ruleville. Within a few days of her moving there nightriders shot up the house where she was staying, missing her. It was impossible to intimidate Mrs. Hamer and she became the heart and soul of the civil rights movement in Ruleville. Her powerful and beautiful voice dominated the mass meetings, which were held more than weekly at the Williams Chapel. She got many people to go down to the courthouse, but none were successful in registering.

Soon she became a state leader in SNCC attending meetings beyond the state. During the return bus ride from one of those meetings in June 1963, at a stop in Winona (about an hour's drive from Ruleville), Fannie Lou Hamer was hauled off the bus by cops, jailed and savagely beaten almost to the point of death. It took her a month to recover. For us she was an awesome inspiration. She was forty-seven at the time, about the age of our mothers, and she exuded love and affection to all the civil rights workers. Sometimes she worried about our safety, and other times she inspired us to find the courage to go forward. She was fearless herself, yet kind and understanding and always ready to listen. Virtually everyone in the black community looked up to her, as did the volunteers. With Charles McLaurin in the two years from 1962-1964 she had forged a special relationship and partnership that lasted her whole life.

Charles McLaurin speaking to a participant in the January 4 demonstration at Indianola. McLaurin never lost an opportunity to educate and strengthen everyone he spoke to. Modest, yet a person of commanding presence, his leadership was indispensable to the project.

Between the two the black community was well organized and they essentially functioned as an alternate government. The mayor of the much smaller white community across the highway did nothing positive for the majority of his citizens and, except for his night-rider cohorts, was not a presence in the community. The nightriders came by mainly at times of mass meetings with their signature pickups with the prominent rifle racks. Late at night there would be occasional shootings of houses of prospective voters. This seemed only to solidify the quiet determination and courage of the black residents. Something of a standoff ensued for a year and a half prior to the summer project; there was no progress in voting rights, but the black community was not in the slightest intimidated.

Our arrival was to signal an attempt to break the stalemate, and Dorrough was extremely hostile to us, as he openly told the reporters who interviewed him, but he took no overt action due to the extensive media attention. Some of his cronies were not so circumspect;

on June 25, a few days after our arrival nightriders firebombed the church. But they were not too competent; the damage was minimal, and the meetings went on as usual. Charles McLaurin had us volunteers canvass the neighborhood to document all the violence and intimidation that had gone on in the past. The worst incident had occurred on the same night the nightriders attempted to kill Fannie Lou Hamer; the home of Herman and Hattie Sisson was targeted and two young Jackson State students were severely wounded while watching TV. When the SNCC worker Charlie Cobb visited them in the hospital, Dorrough arrested him. He claimed Cobb did the shooting as a publicity stunt. We talked to the people, documented all these and countless other incidents, and the accounts were compiled by our highly competent communications director, Dale Gronemeir. Nothing we found was news to McLaurin, but it was a good education for us.

On June 24 Charles McLaurin had bundled thirty of us from Ruleville off to the larger town of Drew, about ten miles north. Half of us were volunteers, the other half were teenagers, and I was asked to drive one of the cars. The media followed us and took pictures and filmed the event for TV. We went door to door in the black neighborhoods, where we were greeted hospitably, but nobody committed to registering to vote. The reason was obvious: the police chief and some armed white citizens followed our every move and took careful note as to who was talking to us. The blacks told us they had been warned previously to have nothing to do with us, above all not to register to vote. The fear was palpable, but no action was taken against us, given the media attention. It was important for McLaurin to "break" Drew, given that in three years he had had no luck in this fear-ridden town; he planned to go back the next day. But Stokely Carmichael arrived with the news that we were confined to Ruleville before we were to go in the afternoon and the plans were put on hold. McLaurin decided in the interim while we were confined to quarters that obtaining a place for a mass meeting in Drew would help break the logjam of fear and he worked through contacts to achieve that. But in the meantime we remained in Ruleville and a few days later the Freedom School teachers arrived.

Since Carmichael's visit everyone had been feeling a little confined and frustrated so the minister, who had been assigned to Ruleville by the National Council of Churches to look after our spiritual wellbeing, offered to organize an ice cream and soda afternoon party for us. When I heard the news of this event I must have made a disapproving face involuntarily; John Harris, who had the same reaction as I, caught my glance and took me aside. He proposed going to the edge of the black community where he had heard there was a place that had available libations of a considerably stronger order than would be available at the minister's party. We went together and although we missed the ice cream social we had a very good time with the denizens of the said establishment, who were most welcoming to me. As for John and me, we became close friends for that summer and for life. The minister was a very well-meaning guy; he attempted to go to church services at the white Methodist church that Sunday, but was turned away. A Methodist minister wasn't even allowed in the local Methodist church because he was told he was living with black people. This was Mississippi in 1964!

The three other volunteers that I remember being closest to those first weeks were Dale Gronemeir, George Winter and Charley Scattergood. Dale was probably a bit older than I. He had been a national secretary for the Committee to Abolish the House Un-American Activities Committee (HUAC). Then he had been a leader of the teachers' union in Berkeley. He drove a motorcycle, although initially he did not bring it to Mississippi, but left it in Memphis. He came with Tracy Sugarman and roomed with him. Tracy was a well-known artist and not quite twenty years our senior. He was under contract for CBS and *Saturday Evening Post* to produce drawings and reportage of the project. Unlike the other reporters, who stayed in motels, Sugarman and Dale stayed with a black family in Ruleville. Dale was brilliant as the communications director. Every day he had a press release that was so professional the reporters would often use it almost verbatim. I learned quickly to report everything that happened to Dale and he would put out a press release. The reporters were eating out of his hand. George Winter was the same age as I, both of us twenty-four; the majority of voter registration volunteers were around twenty-one or twenty-two. He came from California, was quiet and had a sardonic sense of humor. We hit it off immediately; he was housed very close to me, so we often walked the streets together. Charley Scattergood was destined to become very close to me in the following year. He came from Washington but, like Winter, didn't seem to be currently enrolled in school. He was a year or two younger than I. In the long run I came to appreciate him as fearless, intelligent and disciplined.

I also remember Len Edwards, most famous for being the son of a congressman, but a modest and dedicated worker who accepted the inevitable publicity as good for the project, but would probably rather have worked with some anonymity. He attended the University of Chicago, although his father represented the Santa Clara area in California. Gretchen Schwartz, twenty years old, from Swarthmore was dynamic and courageous in every instance. Others were Mike Yarrow, Dennis Flannigan from the University of Washington and Donna Howell from the University of New Mexico, who was the feature of a front-page article in *Look;* I also remember them, but not well. Gretchen and Donna were housed with the Sissons, the house where two young black students had been shot and severely wounded. It was a testimony to the courage of these two to stay there; thanks to them the story of the shooting also finally got to be national news, although two years late.

John Harris had been president of the SNCC chapter at Howard University in Washington, DC. He was originally from Birmingham, Alabama, and majored in chemistry at this the most prestigious of black universities. He quickly got involved in the local struggles and sit-ins. Maryland at the time still had many segregated facilities. (I remember in the summer of 1961 seeing a sit-in at the White Tower hamburger chain in Baltimore, when I worked for General Electric as a summer intern. It was the first sit-in I had ever seen and someone had to explain to me what was going on. It is telling that in 1961 Baltimore, Maryland, still had segregated restaurants.)

John was heavily involved in the struggles to desegregate the eastern shore of Maryland, which were led by the SNCC chapter at Howard. Glen Echo, the chief amusement park in Maryland, was segregated—this in 1962. Much of John's weekends were spent trying to desegregate that place. Other activities involved going to the Kennedy Justice Department in Washington and asking for some action on civil rights. High-ranking officials often received the SNCC members politely and listened to them sympathetically but did absolutely nothing. Stokely Carmichael was then the president of the Howard chapter of SNCC. When his term was up he wanted Cleve Sellars to be his successor, but John was by then so popular that he beat Sellars in the election. Neither Charles McLaurin nor John Harris were great fans of Carmichael, who was ostensibly Mac's superior, but that summer everyone worked together, Harris as Mac's deputy, Sellars as head of the Holly Springs project, Carmichael as head of the very large Greenwood project and district director, and McLaurin as head of the Ruleville project. In practice, however, Charles McLaurin reported directly to Bob Moses.

We never saw Carmichael after that day in June. Greenwood was about forty-five miles from Ruleville and in the next county, Leflore. A big push was made there too, since it had been the focus of so many efforts in the previous three years. They had twice as many volunteers as we had and Stokely was a militant and aggressive leader. There were to be a large number of arrests in that town that summer, but the level of community involvement and the tight organization of the black community that existed in Ruleville and later in Indianola were never duplicated in Greenwood. There are many factors, some external to the projects, as to why Sunflower

County was the most successful of the summer projects, but I would rate the dynamic inspiration of Fannie Lou Hamer and the strategic leadership of Charles McLaurin as the two most important keys to our success.

After the Drew attempt McLaurin asked me to be his driver. His license had been suspended in Greenwood months earlier and he needed a driver. I loved to drive and loved even more getting out of Ruleville so I spent many days with him on the road while others remained confined to the town. On a number of occasions we also spent the night at homes of his contacts in nearby towns. I got to meet a few long time local leaders, like Amzie Moore, as well as some SNCC project leaders in neighboring projects to the west and north.

Charles McLaurin didn't live in the Delta for two years by being careless about security. My orders were strict:

- Never tell anyone where we are going or where we had been. (I never have said anything to this day.)
- Don't even tell people when we leave. Disconnect the interior dome lights so we can't be seen when entering and exiting a car. (That was how Medgar Evars had been killed.)
- Never let a car pass you on the highway no matter how fast you have to drive. (His friend Jimmy Travis had been shot in that fashion.) I sometimes had to drive one hundred miles per hour to avoid being passed, but nobody ever passed our car when I was driving. The Mississippi roads although two-lane were quite straight and there was little traffic in that part of the state. One time, however, I lost control and ended in a ditch, but I managed to drive out without a car passing us. That was the one time he was more scared of my driving than about some sheriff passing us, but as a rule he appreciated my driving and soon I had the keys and was in charge of the SNCC car, a donated brand new white Plymouth.
- When he was in a meeting I was to take charge of his gun. (Yes, Charles McLaurin was armed and usually carried a

revolver in the car. At night he would take it with him, and it was either under his pillow or mine.) He instructed me how to use it and, of course, that I was never to let anyone know anything about it. The project was publicly and officially non-violent, but even among blacks in Mississippi guns were ubiquitous and at least a few project leaders took their cue in that regard from the local people. But it wouldn't be smart to let the press or the local whites know about it. It must be emphasized that it was perfectly legal for anyone to carry a gun in the car and to have weapons in your home. Such was (and still is) the gun culture in Mississippi that gun ownership was one of the few areas where blacks were not discriminated against.

The rides were for me a great political education. Mac told me a lot about his life of activism in Mississippi. He had been skeptical about the project bringing in so many white students, but Fannie Lou Hamer's enthusiasm for the project weighed heavily with him, and he never doubted his ability to command the white volunteers. He grew to like many of us and although he was not demonstrative in any way, one could not help but feel his affection, and he would always be loyal to all of us. He was my age, had come from Jackson and been in the army. There had been little chance of a career for him in Jackson and he started hanging out at the SNCC office. It was Lawrence Guyot who recruited him and convinced him to go up to the Delta. He had never been there before and was reluctant to leave the relative safety of Jackson for the rural areas, but when he arrived in 1962 his intelligence quickly recommended him to the other SNCC veterans. He was a smart organizer, a man of uncommon bravery, able to think strategically but at the same time he was a brilliant tactician. Above all he understood the people he worked with and thus could make use of everyone's abilities. He grew to become quite an inspiring speaker at the meetings or one to one. He was also a deep thinker and I found his analyses of the politics of the country and the movement very much the same as mine.

One day on our weekly trip to Jackson Mac and I stopped at the Billups Gas Station just outside of Ruleville on Highway 49. Normally we filled up in Jackson, but we were low on gas and had no choice but to give our business to the local racist hangout. As we were filling the tank a couple of young white guys sauntered up to us; they were smiling so we sensed no serious trouble.

Ignoring me, they went up to Mac and said, "You are from Mississippi, right?" Mac said "yeah." (Mac never, ever said "yes sir" to white guys.) "Well why don't you have a Confederate Flag sticker on your car?" All the whites in Mississippi did. Mac replied: "That's the flag of racism, slavery, and treason." I was watching their faces as he replied. The grins weren't fazed by "racism," but faded slightly after "slavery," however their jaws dropped to their chests and their mouths hung open after "treason."

They had never heard that before. The state propaganda had portrayed us civil rights workers as the traitors; the whites were supposed to be the patriots defending the Southern or American way of life—they equated the two. Indeed, growing up, I, myself, had always been taught that the Confederate Flag was just a harmless symbol of regional pride. What a history lesson for me in just three words!

We also drove frequently to Jackson, three hours south of Ruleville, where McLaurin made a weekly report to Bob Moses. I was always allowed to sit in on those meetings; such was the democratic and open style of SNCC. I suppose I could have even offered my opinion, but did not do so. Moses generally just listened to Mac and sometimes asked questions; he never gave orders and it often took some subtlety to even discern what his opinion was. But at one of those meetings he let it be known it was okay for the volunteers to venture out of Ruleville, although it took McLaurin to translate his Delphic remarks to me on the way home.

The next day and many days thereafter were taken up with transporting prospective voters from Ruleville to the courthouse in Indianola, twenty-five miles down Highway 49. As the driver of the SNCC car I made the trip each day, often twice or more. One of the voter registration volunteers would come with me as well as a car packed with prospective registrants. In those pre-seatbelt days there was no legal limit to the number of passengers we could fit. And the highway patrol had no interest in vehicle safety. Occasionally Tracy Sugarman lent his rental car to take more. Rarely would a local person loan a car. Very few black people in Ruleville owned cars and those who did had cars in very poor condition, which was okay for transporting workers to pick cotton. But had the vehicle been used for voter registration transport it would have been subjected to a most rigorous inspection by the highway patrol or sheriff and surely impounded.

So it largely fell on me to transport would-be voters. As such I got to know the highways well, the other volunteers well, the media well (which followed us from Ruleville to Indianola, at least for the first few days) and the sheriff better than I desired. The latter was there in Indianola to direct the show and make a display to the media as to how he was protecting us and the prospective registerees. He was well informed about us from his FBI buddies and knew my name and where I was from the first time I set eyes on him. His name was Bill Hollowell; he was a short stocky man in his thirties, but largely bald; he had a decent sense of humor and he liked to tell all and sundry how he hoped I would soon return to my studies at UCLA. Indeed Hollowell wanted all of us to return speedily whence we had come and had in truth no interest in violence being done to us. His ambition, which he once confided to me, was to become an FBI agent and to be a serious applicant his hands had to remain bloodless and he had to demonstrate an ability to keep the lid on.

A year or so before Hollowell had been in a nasty election campaign for the post of sheriff. He had been the favored candidate of the big plantation owners and the businessmen of the county. His opposition, one Parker, a more stereotypical sheriff type—big pot belly and small head, and quite mean looking—was the candidate of the more ignorant class of whites, who often made up the Ku Klux Klan. White violence in Mississippi could easily be turned on their fellows and during the campaign Parker and his gang reportedly waylaid Hollowell and tarred and feathered him, a form of torture peculiar to the US west and south. Hollowell won anyway and in the singular manner of Mississippi politics made Parker his chief deputy. But the morose Parker, who was also often present at the courthouse, had to follow orders and not his instincts and, while he made himself as obnoxious as possible to us, he did us no harm at that point. I did have to drive carefully around the town and park legally at the courthouse, as there would be little chance of avoiding a ticket if I made any driving mistakes. On the highway back the police were invisible; neither speed nor safety was a priority for the Mississippi Highway Patrol, and thus I could drive as fast as I wanted.

In Sunflower County only 114 out of 19,000 eligible blacks were registered as voters. There had been a few more before 1955, but many blacks in the decade preceding that summer had been forced off the registration rolls. (In one county black registration had been purged from 1,221 in 1955 to 71 in 1964; that happened right here in the USA, well advertised as the greatest democracy in the world.) The ride to the courthouse (the only place in the county where one could register) was long and tense; the lines of prospective voters moved very slowly and stretched down the steps and onto the sidewalk in the hot July days. Our hopeful voters were only allowed in the "colored entrance" located in the back of the courthouse, so our long lines didn't inconvenience any whites who may have had business at the courthouse. Carloads of local whites drove by shouting profanities at the group of mostly elderly women dressed in their Sunday best. At noon the registrar would take a long lunch with his buddies in the segregated café across the street; he and the deputies and the local whites, who had entertained themselves that morning insulting the prospective voters, passed a pleasant hour or more while we waited. We bought some soft drinks from a vending machine for us and the hopeful voters and we all waited for His Majesty's return.

We volunteers had the prospective voters well prepared for the twenty-one-question application and coached them on the way up the stairs and through the imposing doors. But the registrar would not let any of the volunteers in the room while he questioned the applicants as to their interpretation of a particular line in the Mississippi constitution. The registrar was as nasty and rude as possible to us and to the blacks who attempted to register; he denied every single black applicant that summer out of the hundreds who had made the courageous attempt. He had to hold his tongue, however, since he was the subject of a lawsuit being prepared by Justice Department lawyers. We met these lawyers at the courthouse too; they were looking for particularly egregious violations. One of the lawyers asked me why I was taking illiterate people to register. He said: "No court will ever rule that illiterates have the right to vote." I said that we believed that every citizen should be allowed to vote regardless of literacy, which was hard to define in any case. Also I pointed out that many illiterate whites were registered. He thought about that, investigated and later when he presented his case in federal court he proved just that. In the end ten months later the settlement of the lawsuit did just as we had asked and a federal judge ordered the registrar to allow everyone to vote regardless of literacy.

Of the twenty-one questions some asked about employment and employers and others about addresses. The answers to these were quickly shared by the registrar and almost immediately any employed applicants were fired from their jobs and others evicted from their homes. The local racist rag would often publish the names of those attempting to register. Since this had been the pattern for two years, the black people of the county were wise to this tactic and almost all of our prospective voters were unemployed; ninety percent were women and they owned their own homes or rented from other blacks. But there were more than a few that summer who lost their jobs or were kicked off the plantation for registering to vote.

The media were also at the courthouse in full flourish with photographers and cameras rolling. I had a lot on my mind and did not pay them a great deal of attention, but in line with SNCC policy I gladly gave interviews when asked and at some point noted in a letter to my parents that I had had my picture in every one of the four major news magazines and been on two of the three major TV networks. My parents, who wanted me out of there, were unimpressed. The *Look* reporters were the most sympathetic to us and took the most time to get the story straight. They spent nearly a month with us; the others were there just for a few days. At one point Chris Wren, the *Look* reporter, and his photographer, Tom, were chased at ninety miles per hour all the way from Ruleville to their motel in Greenwood by what they feared were prospective assassins. Tom told me the next day that he was far more frightened in Mississippi than he had been a few months previously covering the civil war in Cyprus, dodging Turk and Greek bullets.

Mississippi had five congressional districts; as a one-party terrorist state the elections for Congress and the Senate were never seriously challenged and the state's congressional delegation had extraordinary seniority. For example in the second congressional district, where we were located, Jamie Whitten, an arch-segregationist, "served" over fifty-three years in Congress, rising to head the powerful Appropriations Committee. James Eastland, one of the two senators, owned a huge cotton plantation in which violent tactics were used to keep his black workers submissive. It was located in Sunflower County less than ten miles south of Ruleville; he was a senator over a thirty-seven-year span. In 1956 he became head of the Senate Judiciary Committee, which vetted all federal judges. His cohort, John Stennis, was in the Senate for forty-one years and headed the Senate's Appropriations Committee and Armed Services Committee. The latter rose to prominence in 1936 as a prosecutor of three black sharecroppers who had been tortured to confess to a murder, a case that was eventually voided by the Supreme Court. These Mississippi congressmen and senators had far more power than their numbers would indicate and presidents kowtowed to them, including John Kennedy. Johnson only broke with them after the murders in Neshoba County, when he pushed through the civil rights bill over their fierce opposition. Their power to block legislation was curtailed and the bill sailed through Congress that summer, thanks in large measure to the sacrifice of James Chaney, Michael Schwerner and Andrew Goodman.

Don Edwards of San Jose, California, was a principal sponsor of that bill in the House and he came to Mississippi in early July to show his support of the summer project. SNCC took him to the most dangerous part of the state, McComb, in a Klan-dominated area in the southwest corner, where numerous black civil rights activists had been murdered. Congressman Edwards stayed in the Freedom House there. It was bombed after he left, injuring two SNCC workers badly.

The one-party, monolithic, statewide structure was not exactly replicated at the local level, where the Ku Klux Klan vied with the White Citizens' Councils (WCC) for domination. The WCC believed in economic sanctions, police arrests and some measure of non-lethal intimidation as a means to prevent any desegregation or black voting and to scare the volunteers into leaving the state. (The WCC had been founded in Indianola in 1955 and quickly spread throughout the state.) The Klan, which often dominated the most rural parts of the state isolated from the general economy, believed in the tried and true, traditional methods of lynchings, murder and arson. Both groups were present in Sunflower County, but in that summer the WCC held sway.

After leaving McComb Don Edwards went to Jackson, and then he came to Ruleville, where his son was a volunteer. He arrived during the day and snubbed Mayor Dorrough, who cynically wanted to greet him. We volunteers were gathered in front of the Freedom School, which he wanted to see. He came over and spoke to all of us, shook our hands and was most encouraging. He was especially warm to those of us from California. As we were outside talking with him, we were surprised to see Sheriff Hollowell, Deputy Parker and three other deputies arrive and quietly take positions around us and the church, where there was soon to be a mass meeting. We had never seen them in the black quarter before and never so polite. Soon a car arrived with three other congressmen: Ryan from New York and Burton and Hawkins also from California. At the packed meeting there was the normal singing and speeches, then the congressmen were introduced and made brief remarks; they had all been major sponsors of the Civil Rights Bill. Hawkins, the only black member there, spoke at length about his experiences of discrimination in Los Angeles. The crowd could easily connect with him and the reality that a black man could serve in Congress resonated, since Fannie Lou Hamer was a candidate to replace the racist Whitten in the black-majority second congressional district. The meeting was a high point for Ruleville that summer and went on until all of us, congressmen, volunteers and black citizens, joined hands and sang many rousing choruses of "We Shall Overcome."

As we left the church I couldn't help smirking at the deputies, standing guard outside. It was July 7, 1964, my birthday. I had just turned twenty-four.

4

The Standoff in Drew

....

Now does he feel
His secret murders sticking on his hands
Now minutely revolts upbraid his faith-breach…
Now does he feel his title
Hang loosely about him, like a giant's robe,
Upon a dwarfish thief.

MACBETH

That summer the mayor of Drew, Mississippi, William Oliver Williford, and his sullen police chief could feel their oppressive little kingdom shaking. Since 1957 both the mayor and his sidekick had terrorized the black citizens, who were a big majority of the population. A new culture of hope had taken hold in Ruleville and they dreaded its spread north. North of Ruleville by just a few miles, the countryside around Drew was changing from plantations to backwoods-type small farms and the political domination from the White Citizens' Council to the Ku Klux Klan. In the eighty-two years leading up to that summer the state had recorded 539 lynchings of blacks in the state of Mississippi; indubitably this official number is just the tip of the iceberg, as it was difficult to drain a river or swamp in that state without turning up some unidentified bodies. The last officially recorded lynching in 1955 was of Emmett Till, a fourteen-year-old who was murdered just fifteen miles up the highway from Drew for allegedly whistling at a white woman. Some of these murders were carried out by the Klan as part of its regular activities, others by drunken mobs of white citizens, others by young whites just having fun on a Saturday night; some lynchings were by law enforcement officials claiming to want to save the county the trouble of prosecution.

We don't know if Williford or his police chief were Klan members or to what extent the Klan exerted control over the town, but we do know that the mayor and the police chief terrorized the black citizens of their town and allowed nobody to register to vote or even talk to SNCC workers. They darkly looked down the highway at Ruleville, where forty civil rights workers lived in the black section, conducted Freedom Schools with five dozen or more enthusiastic young participants, and where dozens of black citizens had made the trek to Indianola to register, and Williford vowed that this would never come to pass in Drew, whatever means it took.

There was one town where blacks had political power: Mound Bayou. Its population was all black, and it was located about fifteen miles from Ruleville to the northwest. Prior to 1955 some of the leaders of the civil rights movement had come from Mound Bayou, but the repression of the NAACP by the White Citizens' Council had been so severe that many of these early pioneers had been forced to leave the state or drop their activity. The 1964 leaders of the town, fearing for their tenuous lease on this smidgeon of self-government, would have nothing to do with the civil rights movement so there was no project there. We visited the town in early July. Charles McLaurin, Tracy Sugarman, Jeff, another volunteer, a teenager from Ruleville and I drove up there to meet Amzie Moore, long-time NAACP leader in the area and now SNCC's most trusted friend of that earlier generation of civil rights activists. Moore had been one of those early pioneers from the 1955 period who refused to surrender and somehow survived. He had his own business and home so he couldn't be pressured that easily. He took safety precautions very seriously so he was still alive.

We joined Lois, an SNCC veteran from Cleveland, and went to a church in Mound Bayou for a mass meeting, but the attendance sharply contrasted with what we were used to in Ruleville: the church was about the same size, but nearly empty. We from Ruleville occupied the front seats, while maybe a dozen or so local blacks hung out tentatively in the rear. Amzie spoke at the meeting and made the best of it. He was enormously respected in these Delta counties, but the fear of the local people was palpable and for good reason. Mac and other SNCC veterans relied on him for contacts. Lois was looking for a Freedom School location in Cleveland and Mac wanted a place for us to hold mass meetings in Drew. After the meeting Moore indicated he would work on these requests. The problem was, of course, that any structure used for civil rights activity was likely to be burned down. (No less than thirty-seven

Amzie Moore speaks to a meeting in Mound Bayou. Civil Rights Workers are in the front, Charles McLaurin with the fan and author Jim Dann, behind him. A few hesitant local residents are in the back. Amzie Moore effectively founded and maintained the NAACP in the Delta. After the severe repression of the late fifties drove most NAACP leaders out, he refused to be cowed and survived. When the SNCC workers arrived in 1962 he was there to provide contacts and meeting places for them.

black churches were burned down in the state before the summer was through.)

Having a presence in a local community involved having a place to meet regularly, where the local people could draw strength from each other, and feel safe talking to civil rights workers. People like Williford understood this well and were intent on absolutely denying a location for either meetings or Freedom Schools. Tremendous economic pressure, intimidation and threats were used against blacks who might be even considering allowing the use of their private property for us; if this didn't work arson was available. During the previous week, there had already been some arson attempts in Ruleville, but none were successful.

We voter registration volunteers tended to think of ourselves as being on the frontlines and we saw the majority of volunteers, who were Freedom School teachers, as being in the rear. In retrospect, however, I would say the opposite was the truth in terms of transformative power that summer. What I missed, but what white racists instinctively recognized, was that it was the cultural revolution engendered in the Freedom Schools that most threatened their dominion. No doubt it was the Freedom Schools, community centers and the culture of integration and empowerment of local people that Freedom School teachers brought to the communities that caused the greatest fear to Williford and his ilk.

In Ruleville Liz Fusco set up a school with about sixty regular young students; in addition many adults of all ages attended literacy classes. Academically, these were better classes by far than the students had ever seen in their segregated schools. More importantly the teachers taught subjects that were taboo, like black history, the true story of the Civil War and Reconstruction, current events and cultural subjects like art and dance, which had been reserved for whites in Mississippi. The most important thing was that young white people were treating the young black students with respect. This was unheard of in Mississippi in those days. To look a young white woman in the eye was a hanging offense for a young black

A play written and put on by the Freedom School in Indianola. Students often wrote plays and performed them for the community. This one mocks the plantation-owners and their pretended chivalry.

man, never mind to engage and debate with her. The teachers had the students call them by their first names, while the adult blacks were always Mr. and Mrs. This was a powerful day-to-day challenge to the Mississippi way of life and really turned the cultural world in black Ruleville upside down. Real interracial friendships based on mutual respect were forged in these Freedom Schools. I think I at least partly understood this and in my voter registration work I tried to replicate the style of the Freedom School teachers. A number of Freedom School teachers were regular teachers from the North on summer vacation; they universally reported far more satisfaction and learning progress in the Freedom Schools than in the regular schools back home.

The kids who attended these schools were very enthusiastic about the project and aided the voter registration efforts. The most activist—almost all young girls—accompanied us around town and to Drew. I remember as the two main leaders Ora Doss and her sister, Ruby. The kids almost immediately named me "Jim Dandy" from a popular song by the blues singer Lavern Baker. McLaurin was quite amused by this and the name stuck throughout the summer. I kind of liked the attention and it was a bit flattering. There was a verse in the song: "Jim Dandy to the rescue."

The best Charles McLaurin was able to get for a meeting place in Drew was the outside yard of a black church. So one July afternoon he, I, Fannie Lou Hamer, Ora Doss and some friends, as well as some other volunteers piled into a couple of cars for our first mass meeting in Drew. We were joined at the last moment by Judy Collins, the famous folk singer, who was visiting in Ruleville to show support. We from Ruleville made up the bulk of the attendees, but a dozen or so young black men and women from Drew hovered in the background and eventually approached us. The police chief and some other white thugs motored around us with threatening looks. Fannie Lou Hamer spoke inspiringly and I recall Judy Collins's eyes brimming with tears, probably as much for the courage and bravery of the small group as for Hamer's inspiring words. We got out of town before the sun went down.

In the relative safety of Ruleville there was another mass meeting filling the church. Judy and another popular folk singer, Barbara Dane, sang freedom songs led and inspired as always by Mrs. Hamer. After the meeting a few of us volunteers sat outside someone's house with Collins and Dane and sang some more-leftist songs than had been sung in the church. Judy was a popularizer of Bob Dylan and sang many of his songs, which at that time were harshly critical of US society. I remember that night her singing "Masters of War," but she stopped at the last verse: "I hope that you die and your death comes soon, I'll follow your casket on a cold afternoon, and I'll watch as you are lowered unto your deathbed, and I'll stand over your grave until I'm sure that you're dead." She said she had told Dylan she couldn't sing that verse. I had not heard the song before and indicated some perplexity; Barbara Dane, more left than Judy, obligingly sang the verse. I had no problem with the sentiment in the song; nevertheless, I was hugely impressed with Judy's sincerity on that issue as well as her emotion at the rally in Drew in the afternoon. The two folk singers were young and beautiful; they had marvelous voices; for us volunteers it was a magical evening, a break from the tensions of the day. They must have stayed the night with Gretchen and Donna and were gone the next day; they left for other projects or went back North.

The following morning Dale had run off some leaflets announcing another mass rally in Drew for that night. I volunteered to go to Drew to pass them out. McLaurin was busy with some lawyers, who had come from Jackson, so I told Dale I would just go and be back in an hour; Fred Miller and possibly one other person came with me. Fred Miller was the only black volunteer except for John Harris; he was a shy, earnest, thin young man from some college in the upper South; he signed on as a Freedom School teacher, but Mac used him initially for voter registration; later when the schools were in full swing he became a full-time Freedom School teacher, a job in which he excelled. It was already afternoon and the rally was that night. Our plan was to pass the flyers out to some homes where we had previously canvassed and rely on the local people spreading the word. Our idea was to do the job quickly before the police chief even knew we were in town. However, before we got very far the chief did show up in his battered pickup and told me to follow him to what passed for city hall, a ramshackle wooden house. Somehow he had missed Fred. Drew had seen better days; the police chief, whose name I have forgotten, was chief of a force of one, himself; the downtown was mostly boarded up and the mayor's office looked more like a dirty tool shed than a city hall.

I asked if I was arrested; the morose man merely snarled that Mayor Williford wanted to speak with me. The mayor wasn't too unfriendly initially and asked what I was doing; I said leafleting for voter registration. He informed me that black people (he didn't use that phrase) didn't want to vote. I politely disagreed, and he passed onto questions about the Freedom Schools. I explained that they were there to teach literacy and citizenship. I was trying to make the situation seem less threatening to him, but he wasn't buying it. He made no bones about his feeling that blacks (throughout this conversation he used much more insulting nomenclature, which I shan't repeat) were not worthy of schools, voting privileges or citizenship. I debated the point, again politely. Finally his patience was wearing thin with me, but he had to ask the big question that apparently had kept him awake at nights. "What would you think if your sister married one of them?" Once again trying to be mild and polite I said, "If she really loved the man why should I have any objection?" He turned red in the face, stood up and shouted at me: "You are not an American; you are not a white man, you do not have red blood running in your veins." I was taken aback at this sharp turn of events, and thought now I had done it and was headed for jail, but instead the equally angry chief showed me to my car and told me to get out of town and never come back.

Fred had circumspectly waited for me and we drove back to Ruleville and reported the whole thing to Dale, who typically wrote up a major press release. He had the lawyers who were in town on another matter interview me about it. They dutifully took notes. A few days later they had the FBI interview me and Fred. These agents were part of the reinforcements sent in by President Johnson after the Neshoba lynching. They were from North Dakota and were bored by my story. McLaurin found the story amusing, especially the part about red blood.

That evening we did return to Drew. I was there too, despite the chief's warning; we were there to hold our rally outside the church. Somehow we got enough cars to take almost all the voter registration workers there as well as a strong contingent of Ruleville teenagers. There probably were twenty of us from Ruleville. McLaurin

Jim Dann reports to National Lawyers Guild attorneys on the racist diatribe of Mayor Williford of Drew. Fred Miller is in the center with a letter in his pocket. The NLG developed a creative strategy of removing all cases, no matter the charge, to federal court, arguing that a fair trial for Civil Rights Workers in Mississippi was impossible. Several years of legal maneuverings in federal court followed, which effectively prevented any Civil Rights Workers from serving jail time.

led the rally with much singing of freedom songs, chanting and his inspiring speeches. This time some youths from Drew, maybe ten or twenty, approached us and joined in. The chief got out of his car and with a few fellow thugs came closer with the idea of intimidating the Drew people. McLaurin now spoke to the small crowd and asked of the chief and his minions: "What are they afraid of?" The Ruleville girls now took up the singing and sang verses challenging the Drew young men to join in. Now more people from Drew moved to the churchyard and it started getting crowded. Some of the volunteers passed out song sheets. John Harris moved onto the sidewalk to lead the chanting from there. Then the chief lost patience and arrested John, Fred Miller and Mike Yarrow, a white volunteer, for blocking the sidewalk. I wasn't about to let my friends go to jail without me so I looked at the chief and defiantly put my foot on the sidewalk. I imagined that perhaps he had been particularly keen to get me. I, in any event, didn't have time to put a second foot on the sidewalk before he grabbed my shoulder. Before I was arrested I must have handed my keys to someone, but I don't remember whom, probably Charles McLaurin. More or less simultaneously with my arrest Charley Scattergood, Gretchen Schwartz and another volunteer were also grabbed. Then McLaurin signaled to the rest to stay on the lawn as he asked everyone to take a registration form. But the chief had made his point; nobody from Drew took one.

From the back of the pickup as we were about to be driven away John stood up and shouted, "If you register and vote you won't have to elect stupid public servants like this one," looking at the chief. The rest of us started singing freedom songs as loud as we could. A few blocks away we arrived at our destination: the Drew jail, from where we continued the singing nonstop. It was just a concrete structure with one or two small barred windows. The jail was not even as big as a one-car garage; there were separate cells, but the interior doors didn't function so we were all seven together singing away. We sang every song we knew and then repeated them over and over. Gretchen and Charley led the singing. After a few hours Tracy Sugarman arrived with the chief to get Gretchen; Tracy had worried she might be separated from us and harmed so he used his own money to bail her out. She was anything but grateful to be separated from us and the rest of us missed her. But the six of us remaining continued the singing until way after dark, when exhausted beyond measure we fell asleep on the floor. There may have been some mattresses there; I don't remember.

Probably there never had been a plan for us to be separated and Gretchen would have been safe. The authorities had not planned for this arrest; perhaps the incompetent chief had just lost his temper and now he and the rest of them seemed to be at loose ends as to what to do. No doubt Sheriff Hollowell was called in after the arrest to advise them what to do. The first sign to me that they didn't know what they were doing was that in the morning the chief arrived at the jail with breakfast, clearly a last-minute purchase: there were two hamburgers for each one of us. I hungrily devoured mine. I spent much of that year hungry and remember very well every instance in which I got my belly full; this was one. The chief then moved us to the police station, where we were greeted by Tracy, Gretchen and some lawyers. Tracy had raised bail for us from his contacts in Connecticut. The Council of Federated Organizations or COFO had no bail fund; the idea had always been that the Northern volunteers would supply names and contacts of people who would wire down bail money as needed. I and some others, however, had no bail contacts to supply, so the system did not work all that well. Luckily we had Tracy Sugarman on our side; he always played a big role in getting bail money. In the summer Dale would coordinate the effort with Tracy; as long as not too much money was required, it could be wired down in a day. The bail was usually one hundred dollars per person; so seven hundred dollars could be raised without too much difficulty.

After some attempt to mimic a legal proceeding, with which our lawyers obligingly went along, though it seemed to take forever, they let us go back to Ruleville. It wasn't until noon that we got back, but we were all in very good spirits. The lawyers spent the afternoon interviewing us. Around five in the afternoon. we piled into three cars and headed back to Drew for another rally in the churchyard. This time the enemy was better prepared; the chief had passed out helmets and badges to a half dozen or so local lay-abouts, who lined the street in front of the churchyard, trying to look intimidating. The singing was stronger and McLaurin led the crowd as now dozens of Drew people joined in, not only teenagers, but middle-aged ladies as well. But in short order the chief produced a church official, who, prodded by the chief, declared that the church withdrew its permission to hold the rally there.

The Drew City jail was a small concrete affair with little light. None of the internal doors and cells functioned so all arrestees were crowded together. Nobody stayed more than one night before being transferred to either the County Farm or the Indianola Jail.

McLaurin led us to an empty lot next to the church where we continued the rally stronger in both spirits and numbers. To my surprise Drew people came out of nowhere to join in. For the first time in three days the Drew residents outnumbered the Ruleville contingent. But not long after that a pickup appeared with a white lady and, speaking for her, the chief declared that she owned the vacant lot and wanted us off. McLaurin was defiant as we closed about him to protect him. He continued his speech; the chief again tried to get us off the lot. Growing ever more defiant and confident McLaurin led us into the street. It had been previously planned that John Harris would not get arrested this time and I left my keys with him as I joined McLaurin in the street. There were twenty-five of us in the street, of whom maybe eight to ten were from Drew. The ersatz cops surrounded us but McLaurin wouldn't stop talking. They marched us off to the Drew jail and we were singing and chanting all the way.

This time there were ten women of the twenty-five arrested; two were white volunteers (of course, Gretchen was one), four or five young teenagers from Ruleville and five ladies from Drew. Initially we were all stuffed into the tiny jail. There was standing room only but the singing and chanting was so intense I thought the concrete walls would collapse. After an hour or maybe less a bus appeared and the women were carted off to the jail in Indianola, where they were lodged in segregated cells. There was no danger to them since the women's quarters in the jail were rarely used and the white women had the white wing to themselves. We fifteen men remained in the Drew cell block that night singing and chanting, but after three days of rallies we were all exhausted and we went to sleep earlier than the night before. I don't remember exactly who besides me, George Winter, McLaurin, Yarrow and Scattergood was in the group, but the summer volunteers were probably six to eight of the fifteen, the Drew youths either five or six, McLaurin and one or two Ruleville kids making up the rest.

In the morning I awoke and expected a repeat of what happened the day before, and that we would be out before very late in the morning. I mentioned that to McLaurin, but he warned me that with that many arrests it might not be so simple this time. Nevertheless I couldn't wait for my two hamburgers. Of course, McLaurin was right; twenty-five people meant at least $2,500 (actually it was $4,500), and that was not easy to raise overnight. So in the morning the chief loaded us onto a bus. He then passed out a single hamburger to each of us. I complained loudly to him, "Where is the second hamburger?" For a brief moment I think he was about to apologize then caught himself and told me to shut up. The bus took off and we had no idea where we were going, singing freedom songs all the way. It took about an hour to get us to the county farm in Moorhead in the southern part of the county.

The SNCC plan was to bail us out as soon as possible and then, to prevent the case from going to a local court, the lawyers would remove it to federal court. This unique and aggressive strategy was developed by the lawyers from the National Lawyers Guild who sent dozens of volunteers to Mississippi that summer. The federal court would then have to decide whether we could get a fair trial in Mississippi. This process ended up taking years and in the end was usually settled in order for the town to keep the bail money. The lawyers stayed in Jackson and had to drive up to Ruleville to hear our stories and then go to the nearby federal court in Greenville to file the petition. The NAACP nationally had strongly objected to the Lawyers Guild since the organization originally had been founded with Communist Party help. They demanded that SNCC cut ties with the Lawyers Guild, but SNCC refused and we depended on the lawyers all summer and into the next year. The lawyers were sympathetic, professional and very helpful; often a black lawyer from Jackson would come too, since a member of the Mississippi Bar might be needed. But the first step was always to raise bail, and back in Ruleville, Tracy, Dale and others were frantically working the phones since the sheriff told the FBI that our safety in the county farm could not be guaranteed. The situation that day was even more complicated in that the day we went to the county farm one hundred and eleven people had been arrested in Greenwood during a "Freedom Day" picket. So both bail money and lawyers were in short supply. In the end it took $4,500 to get us out; they had raised the price. McLaurin had a bunch of extra charges laid on him and his bail was much higher than the regular one hundred dollars; in addition those of us who were repeat offenders also had our bail doubled or tripled.

We were locked in this large, dark and dirty barn-like structure with no windows, except near the roof and one locked door. There was very little light from those barred holes in the roof and not enough mattresses for the fifteen of us. The captain of the farm said little to us as he put us in, except to promise to bring some more mattresses. We were to be kept together, which we liked, but totally isolated from the other prisoners. Around two in the afternoon a black "trusty"—a prisoner could earn this "status" by "good work," and then he acted as an unpaid assistant jailer, cook and/ or janitor, duties that easily beat picking cotton in the hot sun— brought us the mattresses and our dinner-lunch: a small cup of beans and a piece of cornbread. That was the food for the day. Mac kept everyone's spirits up; this was his twenty-second arrest; the kids from Drew were the most scared, but Mac settled them down quickly. George Winter had a notebook in his pocket and using that, he and I made a chessboard and pieces and the two of us played chess into the night until it got too dark to see anything and everyone went to sleep. It was so dank and filthy and so per- meated with the smell of rat droppings that some of the volunteers got allergic, and I was kept awake part of the night by their wheez- ing and coughing.

The next morning the black trusty brought us breakfast: black heavily-sugared coffee, five biscuits, some molasses and a piece of bacon. The coffee was awful but seemed to be good for allergies. We tried to talk to the "trusty," but he whispered that he was under orders not to talk to us. However, he did anyway and told us he had been in there nine months. The regular prisoners had to work the cotton fields of the farm from dawn to dusk, often chained and whipped if they slacked off, so for him to get a job as trusty was a real break and he couldn't disobey the captain's orders. Even so he found a way to get cigarettes into the cell for us.

In the meantime the bail money came into the Western Union Office from all corners of the country and was collected by Tracy, Dale and two of the Freedom School teachers. It was brought to Sheriff Hollowell and first the ladies from the Indianola jail were released then cars went out to the county farm to get us. We didn't get our two o'clock supply of beans and cornbread that day since our release was in the works (the captain said nothing to us, but we got a message to that effect from the trusty) and in late after- noon Tracy and two cars showed up to take us home. There was no formal release: we just walked out of the now open door and down the sunbaked path to the gate, where Tracy and the cars were

Church Street in Indianola in 1964. The street had been thriving in the early fifties as a center of black commerce and entertainment for plantation workers. It was the creative headquarters for B.B. King and other Blues singers, but by 1964 it was no longer at its peak.

waiting. Someone kindly thought to bring us sandwiches, of which I devoured more than my share.

It was July 17, 1964, and the trip back to Ruleville took just forty-five minutes. We were fortunate; the Greenwood arrestees would still be locked up in the neighboring Leflore county farm for three more days.

TOWN OF INDIANOLA, MISSISSIPPI

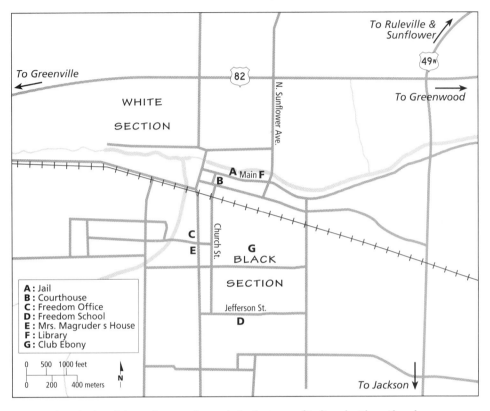

A major breakthrough was to be made in the town of Indianola. The railroad tracks separated the black and white sections.

5

Breakthrough in Indianola

....

Now is the winter of our discontent
Made glorious summer by this sun of York;
And all the clouds that lowered upon our house
In the deep bosom of the ocean buried.
Now are our brows bound with victorious wreaths...

RICHARD III

The welcome we received in Indianola from the enthusiastic black residents was in sharp contrast to the palpable fear that we had initially encountered in Drew. The moment we parked our car on Church Street enthusiastic young people greeted us, happy that the "freedom riders" had finally arrived. And in short order the iron grip of the White Citizens' Council over the black community was shattered and sundered. The organization of Indianola was arguably the Mississippi summer project's greatest victory. Certainly the mass of people that got involved in civil rights in Indianola was nowhere else matched. For this to happen so decisively in the birthplace of the White Citizens' Council tasted delicious to the SNCC veterans, who had worked so hard for more than two years for this denouement.

As much as he would have liked to keep pushing in Drew, Mac realized that it was not practical at that time. With so many still locked up in Greenwood, and our bail contacts already hit to the limit, another mass arrest could have stopped the Sunflower County project cold. (This more or less is what happened in Greenwood.) Moreover, it had always been his ambition to break Indianola. To get a base at the county seat would, if nothing else, make it easier to bring the residents of the northern part of the county down to register. Additionally there were indications that the Indianola residents were ready for us in a way that the Drew people were not. So Drew was put on hold. Later that summer Ruleville voter registration volunteers would canvass Drew again, but for now Charles McLaurin shifted our attention to Indianola. It was not much more than a day or two after we got out of the county farm that McLaurin had me drive him, John Harris, Scattergood and Gretchen the twenty-two miles from Ruleville to Indianola. A small group would be better, he thought, to avoid mass arrests and the bail problems. In November 1963, during the Freedom Vote campaign, fourteen SNCC workers, including Charles McLaurin and volunteers, had been arrested in Indianola just for passing out leaflets in the black section. We had no idea if our reception by the police would be any better than it had been in Drew, or Mac's reception in Indianola eight months earlier, so we were prepared to be arrested that day.

This time I drove past the courthouse, over the railroad tracks that separated the black and white sections, and parked on Church Street in the commercial heart of the black section. (This amounted to half a dozen cafés and very small stores and a car mechanic; the white commercial section located across from the courthouse did not amount to much more, although there was a Piggly-Wiggly supermarket and some clothing and gun stores.) We didn't even have time to get out of the car before the first young people came up to us, welcoming us and volunteering to guide us around town. We canvassed not only them, but with these teenagers as guides went around to houses with our forms that committed people to attempt to register. There were, of course, plenty of negative responses, but the number of positive ones and the growing number of teenagers that almost joyfully accompanied us surprised all, including, I think, Mac.

The police were invisible in the black section, although they watched us warily as we drove through the white section on the way to and from the highway. Indianola was almost unique in Mississippi in that the city in 1949 had hired a black man, Slim Jack, to be the cop responsible for the black section of town. The NAACP, of which Jack was a member, had pressured the city to do it. For the white powers that hiring had the added bonus that the white cops—there were about half a dozen—wouldn't have to be bothered with law enforcement in the black section, which was a low priority for the city. In the late forties and early fifties, there had been quite a striking double standard of law enforcement in that town. Church Street was a very lively nighttime scene with much drinking, gambling and brawling as blacks came in from the countryside to let off steam. It was on Church Street that B.B. King and other blues singers entertained hundreds in those years. The county was legally "dry" in that the sale of alcoholic beverages was prohibited. However, in the black sections of the county black cafés did a thriving business in alcoholic drinks and also sold bottles of liquor quite openly, even to kids. This was allowed for blacks but not for whites, provided the sheriffs and cops got their "cut." The deputies made a prosperous living on the side importing liquor for the black cafés; indeed the provision of liquor to the black cafés was often the chief reason for the vigorous rivalry in sheriff elections in "dry" counties. The main cafés in Indianola were the White Rose Café and Club Ebony, where B.B. King still came to sing occasionally. Before the civil rights movement the white "good ole boys" would come across the tracks to buy their whiskey and rye to drink in their Chevies, which they drove to the levees. But now it would look bad for local whites to come to the black section and they didn't come very much any more. So the whites lived a largely non-alcohol life, very sedate and quite boring in comparison with the blacks.

So as not to interfere with the deputies' business dealings Slim was made responsible for only some minimal level of policing in the black quarter, and only in exceptional circumstances would the white cops come in. Jack had arrest powers over blacks, but not whites. While the blues scene on the street had died down by 1964 and most of the black young men, who had kept the street humming, had left the state, the same general paradigm of double standard for drinking and of separation of police powers held. This helps explain why we had such a free reign in those first days in Indianola. No doubt Slim Jack was watching us to some extent and reporting to his bosses, but he was not a young man any more; he was fifty-five, and he had little energy or enthusiasm to carry out the White Citizens' Council's agenda. We rarely saw him while we were out canvassing.

The next day Mac had me make two trips so more volunteers from Ruleville could join in the canvassing, while John Harris remained behind in Indianola directing the operation. In the afternoon John was able to report a major breakthrough. Mrs. Irene Magruder, who owned a house two blocks from Church Street in a quiet residential area, offered to house the "freedom riders." This courageous act on her part gave us what we were looking for, a place to permanently house our volunteers in Indianola. The house was large with four bedrooms and a phone, and she had no family living with her at the time. Also it was located on a dead-end street, making a raid by nightriders difficult. Mac lost no time in directing John Harris, Charles Scattergood and Gretchen to move in the next day. So the "freedom riders" would now be in Indianola day and night. I would be tasked with bringing in a carload of volunteers from Ruleville to reinforce them every morning and then to return before dark. John was now in charge of the Indianola project, although under the overall direction of Mac. That way Mac was free each day either to stay in Ruleville or go to Indianola as the situation warranted.

The people of Indianola gave us the honorable title of "freedom riders" after the brave SNCC and CORE young men and women

George Winter is canvassing the black community, probably in Indianola. Asking people to risk all by going down to the Courthouse to register to vote was the main day-to-day job of the Voter Registration volunteers. Any employed black was likely to lose his job; a renter could lose his housing and the physical reprisals were often real and potentially fatal. All this risk was asked of the black residents, and everyone, including volunteers, knew that the attempt to register was doomed to fail, at least in the short-term.

who had come in 1961 to integrate the southern bus stations. The Supreme Court had declared in 1960 that continued segregation of interstate buses and station facilities was illegal. In May 1961 the Congress for Racial Equality or CORE led a freedom ride of two buses from Washington, DC, bound for New Orleans. The Border States and places like Virginia were able to accept the law and the desegregation of the buses, but by North Carolina hostile mobs appeared and they grew increasingly violent as the rides went on until the buses reached Alabama, where an out-of-control mob burned down a bus and severely beat the passengers. A second bus upon arrival in Birmingham was met by a vicious mob of thugs and police, led in person by the police commissioner; the bus was damaged and the passengers were beaten to within an inch of their lives. CORE was ready to quit the project after that, but SNCC students stepped in from black colleges in the South and vowed to continue the ride to Jackson, Mississippi. The Kennedy Administration was opposed to the rides despite the government's obligation to uphold court rulings, and was quite willing to let white southerners defend their way of life no matter what happened to the freedom riders. But the horrific attack on the private property of a major US corporation galvanized John Kennedy into action. Pressure was put on SNCC and CORE to abandon the rides; when that didn't work a deal was apparently made with the Alabama and Mississippi authorities that if they protected the buses from damage when the freedom riders arrived in Jackson they could be dealt with any way the state saw fit.

The state saw fit to send the freedom riders to Parchman State Penitentiary for forty days each; they were kept under conditions that would have made any contemporary Mideast dictatorship blanch. The rides kept coming, however, as the conscience of many young people, black and white, was aroused. Eventually, though, the harsh repression was too much and the Mississippi authorities had their way in the near term. But the long-term reverberations were unfavorable to the authorities, as many of the freedom riders did not leave the state after their term in the pen was up. Instead they hooked up with young black students in Jackson to try to desegregate that city. Attempts to open up the state fair for blacks and the city library in Jackson were met with harsh repression. The state then moved to attack all blacks up and down the state, using increasingly harsh economic and police methods.

The Kennedy Administration had been busy in its first year in office using its famously great eloquence to attack the Soviet Union for its lack of human rights, and it was committing troops and resources to fight for "freedom" in Vietnam and Cuba. Now Kennedy found himself embarrassed by all this bad international press about the lack of human rights in the American South. So it was in this context that the Voter Education Project was adopted with the idea of curtailing direct action in favor of the slower and out-of-sight process of voter registration. The NAACP as well as most Mississippi black leaders favored this approach too since the direct action had so inflamed the ignorant white mobs that nobody was safe any more. So SNCC in 1962 started its voter education drives, first in Klan-ridden southwest Mississippi, but the murder of local leaders there forced SNCC to leave that area for the Delta in late 1962.

There with the guidance and contacts of long-time local NAACP leaders like Aaron Henry in Clarksdale and Amzie Moore in Bolivar County, who had led various civil rights actions in the past, the SNCC workers had a better chance. Bob Moses and his group, some of them ex-freedom riders, put down roots in Clarksdale and Cleveland, then expanded their operations to the fiercely repressive town of Greenwood, and in short order were welcomed by the black community of Ruleville in Sunflower County, the heart of the Delta. Greenwood, the largest town in the Delta, was twenty-four miles to the east of Indianola and in early 1963 had seen a massive attempt by SNCC to build a movement. After the first arrests Moses called for all SNCC hands to come to Greenwood. McLaurin came from Ruleville to take part and there were many arrests and shootings. But in the end there was a base set up in Greenwood and a small amount of progress in voter registration, though little progress in ending the violent repression. However, arrests, shootings, arson and bombings didn't stop SNCC and by mid-1963 the SNCC workers were in Greenwood and Ruleville—twenty-five miles north of Indianola—to stay and there was a small project in Greenville, twenty-four miles west of Indianola. The SNCC workers passed through Indianola many times in 1963 and 1964 and sometimes stopped to canvass, but with neither lodging nor a meeting place in the city McLaurin and his comrades had no permanent presence. As the Ruleville prospective voters made the trek to the county courthouse in Indianola the residents of that city noticed and watched their Ruleville compatriots, waiting for the "freedom riders" to set down roots in Indianola. Knowing who the original freedom riders were and what they had gone through I was both a little embarrassed and very flattered by the appellation.

The Mississippi Delta is the northwest corner of the state consisting of about ten counties bounded by the Mississippi River on the west and some of its main tributaries on the east. (See map on page 51.) For ten thousand years the rivers had periodically flooded the land, leaving behind some of the richest soil to be found in the United States. Forests covered the area and in their midst Native American farming civilizations had at one time taken root, although these farms had disappeared before the white settlers came with their slaves around 1815. Slaves cleared some of the rich forests and large cotton slave plantations marked the land until 1865. During the Reconstruction the Delta plantations were broken up and many independent black and white farmers got land. Through a combination of economic pressure and Klan violence most independent farmers had their land taken away by the end of the nineteenth century and plantations on an even more massive scale than in slavery times dominated when we arrived. Many of the forests were cleared and the plantation owners forced blacks into a semi-feudal state of dependency, called sharecropping. The cotton monoculture by the time we got there dominated the landscape and the economy. After World War II sharecropping was largely replaced by a system of paid day labor, and the population of the Delta was close to seventy-five percent black.

During the fifties tractors were finally introduced by the plantation owners, who, with such a reservoir of cheap black labor, had little incentive to innovate. Even in 1964 the Mississippi plantations were way behind other cotton-growing regions like Texas and California in the use of modern equipment. Cotton picking was still entirely done by hand; the rate was three dollars for a hundred pounds. You had to work very hard to earn more than three or four dollars a day at that rate. (Once Charley Scattergood and I tried our hand at cotton picking on some land owned by the Black Baptist Association. We worked very hard for an afternoon and, paid at the going rate, earned less than forty cents.) The segregated schools had different schedules; the black schools had vacation when the cotton was ready to be picked, so that black kids would be available for the picking. This was a strong economic reason for the plantation owners to oppose integration of schools. In the early spring the tractors were used for planting and young black men could earn five dollars a day driving a tractor. Later in the spring chopping (hoeing) was done to clear the weeds; this earned three dollars a day. For all these tasks truckloads of black laborers were brought to the plantations. Some sharecropping remained for those owners who wanted more control by having their laborers on site and always available, but most preferred the day labor system as the more profitable. A constant sight that summer was the rinky-dink trucks plying the highways, overflowing with black people on the way to the plantation.

Sunflower County was in the middle of the Delta and the economy was, despite the name, entirely cotton. The big plantations dominated the flat land and each extended for miles as far as the eye could see. In the residual woods off the beaten tracks there were still a number of small farms, some owned by whites and some by blacks. In the towns there were cotton gins to remove the seeds, and in Indianola and a few other places cotton baling plants. These firms employed whites as mechanics, managers and in the skilled trades, and black men as laborers. The whites also worked in the small commercial establishments and as overseers and cops. But in general there was not much economic need for whites, and they only made up about twenty percent of the population of the county. The plantation owners relied upon the poor whites to control the black majority, but otherwise the economy had little use for them. The whites were often idle and indolent, and usually abysmally ignor-ant. The black people, though poorly educated, were by contrast in general hardworking, much more aware of what was going on in the world and they had a very rich and lively cultural life.

Besides working in cotton a few blacks owned stores, repair shops or funeral parlors, and some were teachers and ministers. People employed in the latter two occupations tended to be the most conservative since they made more money than their neighbors, and it wouldn't take much to antagonize the ruling powers who might force them to leave relatively cushy jobs to end up picking cotton.

Finding a place for mass meetings in Indianola was now for us the biggest priority, but the black ministers of the Indianola churches were universally negative to our inquiries. You couldn't blame them since they tended to have more expensive churches than those in Ruleville and didn't want these nice buildings burned down. So as we canvassed we asked their parishioners to put pressure on their pastors to let us use the churches. We were not too hopeful, but within a week we were surprised to be asked to meet with Rev. Kirkland, the head of the county's Black Baptist Association.

Charles McLaurin, John Harris and I went to his house outside Indianola. Rev. Kirkland was a slim man maybe about forty years old, soft-spoken and very intelligent. As the year went on I grew to like him a lot, and I think he liked me. The two of us developed a relationship of trust and mutual respect. He preached at the town of Sunflower and often peppered his sermons with calls for freedom and praise for us civil rights workers; at least he did when I was there. At this meeting he had a proposition for us. If we would agree not to ask to use the churches in Indianola for civil rights meetings, the association would give us a large building on the edge of town that had served in the past as a school, but was not currently being used. The building had a very large meeting hall that could serve for mass meetings and several rooms that could be classrooms and libraries for our Freedom Schools. It was surrounded by about four acres of cotton (that was where I and

Scattergood picked cotton one fall afternoon), but it was within easy walking distance for the whole black part of town, just two blocks from Church Street. This proposition was far better than we could possibly have hoped for and Mac readily agreed. We got the keys that day and within a day or two Liz Fusco was setting up the Indianola Freedom School and Dale was running off leaflets for our first mass meeting in Indianola.

A few days previously on July 20 John and I had been canvassing in the black community and decided that it would be a pleasant lunch break to grab a hamburger at the café across from the courthouse, where we had noticed the deputies and other layabouts normally gathered during the registrar's long lunch break. So we leisurely sauntered into the café and, in short order, were unceremoniously marched out at double time by the owner and a few of his friends. The owner then locked the door and loudly intoned that he was closed for the day. We then went to the White Rose Café in the black section and had an excellent repast. Sad to say the usual customers of the white café didn't have that option and had to go home. The next day driving in I couldn't help notice that the something white café had a big sign that it was now the something "key club" with a prominent brass door lock, although at a cursory glance it appeared that most of the usual customers had keys.

On the afternoon of the first mass meeting we handed out and posted leaflets all over in the black community. It was quite unnecessary since everyone we ran into seemed to know about the meeting before we could even tack up a leaflet. In the afternoon we had some handbills left over and John and I decided it would be a nice gesture to tack some up in the white downtown area. So we posted them on parking meters around the courthouse and on telephone posts in the square. We paid particular attention to the telephone posts on the sidewalk next to the new key club. A young Indianola cop, apparently new to the force that year looked at the posters we had put up, saw we were in the process of putting up more and cleverly deduced that we were responsible for the proliferation of unwanted handbills. The budding young sleuth reported his findings to his superiors and returned just as we were finishing up; he came up to us and said we had to go to the police station. Were we being arrested? No, the chief just wanted to speak to us. So we graciously followed him across the square, and were ushered into the chief's office. The town square was small, and police station, courthouse, jail, post office, Piggly-Wiggly and key club were all on the same block. I must admit the police station was considerably cleaner and better lit than the pigsty in Drew and had comfortable chairs across from the chief's desk. The chief indicated for us to sit down and then dismissed young Sherlock.

Chief Bryce Alexander was a short, stocky and garrulous fellow with beady eyes, quite the opposite of his morose, sallow colleague with sunken eyes in Drew. He seemed to want to impress us with his up-to-date knowledge of the legalities of the new Civil Rights Law, which, he informed us, did not apply to private key clubs like the one across the street. I thought to mention that we deserved membership since we were the impetus to the founding of the key club, but John, remembering SNCC's focus that summer was not desegregation, told him that we were in Indianola to register voters and would not try to enter the key club. He seemed reassured by this, but then went on to explain to us that it was very dangerous to tack up posters on telephone poles, since a lineman trying to climb up a pole might trip on our leaflets. In those days utility linemen actually climbed poles by means of foot-long spikes inserted into pre-drilled holes in the pole. I tried in vain to picture the possibility of a handbill interfering with this process, but John posed a more germane question. John asked why it was only our leaflets, announcing the mass meeting that posed such a danger to a lineman and not all the others already decorating the poles announcing bingos, bazaars and the like in the white churches. The chief was temporarily speechless, but mumbled something to the effect that he would take them all down. (He didn't.) He then guided the conversation to other topics. He asked about the program for the mass

Indianola Police Chief Bryce Alexander, a committed segregationist, guards the entrance to the Indianola Public Library to prevent any blacks from using it. The White Citizens' Council counted on him to maintain the local Jim Crow Laws, even though in late 1964 the federal Civil Rights Act had voided them. While he preferred to avoid overt police brutality and unnecessary arrests, his first priority was to maintain segregation.

meeting; we told him it was for voter registration. He seemed okay with that and didn't even make the usual comment that "they" didn't really want to vote.

I was awaiting the famous question as to whether I wanted my sister to marry one of "them," but it didn't come. Instead the chief seemed intent on impressing us that he was a man of the world. He asked me where I was from; I told him LA. He hadn't been there, but said he had lived in Chicago for three years, looking at John, assuming, since John was black and not from Mississippi, he must be from Chicago. The world traveler chattered on in this vein for some minutes, when John diplomatically asked if he had no further need for our company could we leave. It did seem clear from our little conference that the police had no intention of interfering with the mass meeting that night and in truth that was all we really wanted to know from him. So we were politely escorted out and as we passed the key club on our way back to Church Street we noticed that all our leaflets on the poles and parking meters had already been taken down; there would be no danger to a lineman climbing up the poles that night from our leaflets, although the bingo and bazaar posters still remained a hazard.

On another occasion a few days later I had to see Chief Alexander about something, I can't remember what, maybe a permit or the like. He took me aside and said how much better he liked dealing with John Harris than McLaurin. (He bizarrely assumed, I suppose, that it was up to me to make the choice.) The well-traveled philosopher then had some stupid hypothesis that I won't bother to repeat. He later learned to regret this initial assessment of how easy John was to deal with. I did relate his ridiculous ruminations to McLaurin. But Mac found Alexander anything but amusing and told me although he may talk like a fool, he can be a very mean sort. I eventually was to see the truth of Mac's observations.

On the corner of Church Street John and I passed Scattergood addressing a group of young people. He assured them the mass meeting that night would be safe because FBI agents "with guns" would be guarding us. That was quite a bit of hyperbole, of course, since FBI agents were under orders by their boss never to guard civil rights workers; I mentioned that to Charley after his little talk, but he smiled and said there was always that possibility; Scattergood was a perennial optimist. In any event there was excitement in the air that evening with many people telling us they would be at the mass meeting, but still experience told us not to expect a big crowd. First mass meetings in any town usually were considered a big success if they drew fifteen or twenty local people. We normally ferried a contingent of Ruleville people to boost the crowd numbers, but with me and the SNCC car already in Indianola, there would be no more than one or two carloads from Ruleville to make the meeting look mass. It was due to start at around 7:30 p.m. and Mac would be brought down in Tracy's car; he would be the main speaker. Well before he arrived two hundred local people had already entered the Freedom School and were loudly singing.

John was warming up the crowd. I was outside waiting for Mac and watching for the police. When Mac came and heard the loud singing and saw the crowd, which was still streaming in, he was grinning from ear to ear. The size of the crowd was beyond his wildest hopes and expectations. The sheriff and Chief Alexander arrived about then with a few uniformed white cops; they stayed on the street well outside the school grounds; of course, the promised FBI agents with guns never materialized. The National Council of Churches' spiritual advisor for us that week was a young Rabbi, Alan Levine, who, I believe, had actually called the FBI for protection. I was supposed to watch for the police but was so taken with the excitement of the moment that unknown to me the local black policeman Slim Jack had gone inside; he must have walked just past me. When he was spotted inside the people started shouting "Go, go!" since the young people of Indianola in particular didn't want him there; Jack apparently felt threatened and pulled out his gun, but within a minute or two left the building after being confronted and shamed by Mac. A couple of white cops did at that point approach the door, but only to get Jack safely out of there. Rabbi Levine then went to the sheriff and lodged a complaint with him and the FBI. (The FBI was always happy to take complaints, but only after they got names, addresses and other information from the COFO workers and volunteers making the complaint; no doubt they tossed away the reports of violence we gave them, but forwarded all our personal information to their Washington headquarters with a copy to the local sheriff.)

The singing and chanting never stopped, but only gained in strength. Most of the cops drove off then and the meeting never lost a beat. John introduced Mac to the cheering crowd of three hundred packed into the Freedom School. Mac was energized by the people and launched into a long stem-winder. He told of his first trip to the Delta; how scared he was in that long bus trip from Jackson; the voter drives, the many attempts to come to Indianola, his five arrests in that city. He tied it all in to the organizing for the upcoming Democratic Convention and the need to have a black electorate, to have real police protection, economic benefits and full and meaningful equality. I was spellbound by this, his best speech ever. It was followed by thunderous applause and the singing of freedom songs into the night. John announced the start of the Freedom School the next day and another mass meeting was promised in a day or two.

The next few days there were so many things to do and we were in such a state of euphoria over the meeting that I am not at all sure of the sequence of events. About half a dozen Freedom School teachers moved into Indianola and Liz Fusco had classes begin immediately. The attendance was huge for just starting out, at least seventy-five kids and a number of adults in the literacy classes. They were soon writing poetry, complaining to their teachers about registering to vote and forming a Mississippi Student Union. We were still conducting voter registration classes and escorting people to the courthouse. I had to ferry books and materials from Ruleville to Indianola, and we had to find places for the Freedom School teachers to stay in Indianola. I am not sure of all the housing arrangements; there was some doubling up at Mrs. Magruder's house; some stayed at the Freedom School and we found some other housing in the community. In Ruleville Linda Davis, who was the most dedicated and creative teacher there from the University of Chicago, took over from Liz as head of the Freedom School in Ruleville. There were a number of preparations for the Mississippi Freedom Democratic Party's upcoming challenge to the regular Democrats at the national convention that August. In that period there were organized precinct meetings, mostly consisting of people from Ruleville, and a county convention for the MFDP (Mississippi Freedom Democratic Party). Finally we prepared for the second mass meeting, which would feature Fannie Lou Hamer as speaker. All this entailed constant driving for me back and forth from Ruleville to Indianola, and sometimes if it got late I too stayed at Mrs. Magruder's house.

The second mass meeting was bigger than the first by a factor of two. Some five hundred people came and the school was packed standing room only with many people outside on the steps and in the yard. Luckily Mrs. Hamer's voice was so loud it could be heard outside easily enough. The few cops on the street were treated to her singing freedom songs, although unlike the hundreds of black people they showed no emotion. Her speech resonated completely with the crowd, and applause and interruptions like "Yeah!" and "You tell it!" punctuated her every word and energized her even more. She was quite euphoric as she left Indianola that night. For the third meeting McLaurin called on Jim Forman, executive director of SNCC, to be the feature speaker. It was decided that Forman would speak from the steps to the crowd in the field in front of the school. There may have been close to a thousand people that night. He refuted the charge that SNCC members were outside agitators by turning it around. He said we were "inside agitators, and you know what an agitator is… that's the part of the washing machine that gets all the dirt out. That is what we are here for: to get all the dirt out." The crowd loved it and many pointed to the cops on the street to emphasize what dirt Forman was talking about. By this time many people were coming to the meetings from nearby plantations and towns like Sunflower and Moorhead as well as Indianola. The young people from these towns stayed on with friends to attend the Freedom Schools in the next days. These kids wanted to do more and in the Freedom Schools they discussed the possibility of a boycott of the segregated high school when the term began in the fall.

The huge mass movement in Indianola made selective economic reprisals quite difficult. First because the large crowds gave any one person some anonymity, and second because to punish all the people now involved would have been economically suicidal for the white power structure. In addition to the work in the cotton fields many women worked as maids for the wealthier white families; the wage of three dollars a day was not great, but helpful. Unlike the men the black women were not normally punished for registering to vote or attending mass meetings. The white women employers were not sympathetic to civil rights by any means, but usually the black maids were indispensable as lynchpins of the white household in a way that cotton field workers were not indispensable to the plantation. Thus the maids not only kept their jobs but often were a great source of intelligence for us. Their employers treated them as furniture and spoke in front of them as if they were inanimate. In that way we heard things and got warnings. That would be especially valuable in the fall when the white power structure counterattacked.

In the summer the economic reprisals were nullified by a number of measures that SNCC had taken starting the year before. When in the year before the Leflore County officials made the strategic error of cutting off federal surplus food distribution to black people for their participation in the movement, SNCC organized a massive food drive in the North. They distributed truckloads of food and later clothing in the black community, giving first priority to those who had registered to vote. The food and clothing drives spread to all the movement counties. In the impoverished Delta this was a significant economic influx. In addition we volunteers had been asked to bring one hundred and fifty dollars in cash with us and this was largely given in Sunflower County to the black families that housed us. A huge supply of donated books and school materials made our Freedom Schools better equipped than the regular segregated ones. More food and clothing came during the summer and were distributed in the Freedom Schools. Doctors came from the north to freely treat and vaccinate people. They, the lawyers, press and we volunteers spent money in the black community. We bought our groceries not from the Piggly-Wiggly but at Hollins Grocery Store near Mrs. Magruder's house or Oscar Giles's Penny Savers grocery on Church Street; Giles had been head of the county NAACP for a decade. We ate at the White Rose Café, whose owners were openly sympathetic, and we often went to Club Ebony, which was owned by B.B. King's adopted mother. All of this had a significantly positive impact and the economic sting the White Citizens' Council was used to administering to the recalcitrant blacks was now of little account. The positive cultural and economic impact of the COFO presence in the community, the mass movement, the TV attention and the bad reputation the Mississippi establishment was getting made many feel that the long-awaited change was now around the corner. A new hope was in the air.

Around this time the bodies of Chaney, Schwerner and Goodman were found, and outside of the Deep South there was a furious reaction, not only for the murders themselves but for all the lies and insults that had come nonstop from the elected officials of the state for six weeks. Donations now came in much faster in those days of August. It was especially easy to raise money for security. One day it was announced that the SNCC car was to get a two-way radio, and a man came down from the north to install it. We got a large supply of fire extinguishers for the Freedom School and all the houses in which we were domiciled. To handle the increased correspondence John got a post office box in town, Box 30. We got more mail and money orders than any of the white people in town and the white post office clerks would often glare at us, as did the Western Union people when we cashed those wired money orders. Later, when arrests came, all the arrestees, local or volunteers, were instructed to give as their address, 'Box 30,' much to the chagrin of the cops who would say, "You don't live in a post office box." They, of course, knew were we lived, but it was a nice act of defiance and solidarity for us to stick to that despite the intimidations. We were able at this point to rent a small vacant house close to Mrs. Magruder's to house the extra Freedom School teachers and to use as an office; it was quite safe from nightriders in that it could only be reached by a footpath. It only had two small rooms with no furniture initially, but people made do.

Indianola had a weekly paper, the *Enterprise-Tocsin,* which nobody in the black community read since it was so shrilly racist. But John thought it useful to take out a subscription to keep up with what the enemies were saying, at least to themselves. One day I was surprised to find that almost the whole paper was devoted to me. They had picked up a story from the Jackson daily that had been fed to the White Citizens' Council, probably by the FBI. The story in the Jackson daily was about communist infiltration of the freedom summer. The National Lawyers Guild, of course, was mentioned, but several volunteers who had leftist backgrounds were also the targets of this diatribe, even the martyred Andrew Goodman was not spared. My old roommate Ridenour, the only open communist, who by this time had already left Mississippi, featured prominently and I was mentioned as his former roommate. Only a communist, they figured, would room with a communist. The address of the place where we had lived in Venice was given as if to lend factual authority to the story. And now right here in our peaceful, loving community of Indianola James Dann, suspected communist, was agitating away. For the good old boys in the key club this must have been the talk of the day, but in our project or in the black community at large it went over like a lead balloon. Most people thought that if the *Enterprise-Tocsin* said it, then it must be a lie, and I was never even bothered by any questions about the article. The SNCC leaders had been called "communist" so much that these not-at-all-uncommon instances of red-baiting reporting went unnoticed. Fannie Lou Hamer once remarked in a different context: "If you haven't been called a communist you must not be doing anything." Only the sheriff some time later asked me about the article and I told him not to believe what he read in the *Enterprise-Tocsin*. Even he seemed to grant me that point. Years later that local paper was taken over by young liberal journalists, who became staunch supporters of the civil rights movement. The paper is now the opposite of what it was in those days.

I was privy to another interesting meeting late that summer. McLaurin had me drive him to a nearby town to meet a very close friend of his who had been in the Delta from the start; the two had been strong comrades, sharing jails, beatings and even assassination attempts. This veteran SNCC worker was, however, sitting the summer project out; he had been within SNCC among the staunchest opponents of bringing in a large number of whites, and now, I suppose, felt he owed Mac an explanation. He was a very soft-spoken and earnest man, and friendly to me, although my presence at this meeting was only accidental. I felt myself drawn to his intellect and obvious passion for justice.

He had literature from Robert F. Williams, which he gave Mac. Williams (1925-1996) was known to me; I had read his book, *Negroes with Guns* (1962). As a pioneer in the civil rights movement and head of the NAACP in Monroe, North Carolina, from 1958, Williams had seen the black community subjected to hideous Ku Klux Klan violence. He responded by organizing armed self-defense squads and soon the community was heavily armed. The cowards in the Klan stayed away and it worked for three years. But in 1961 police and the FBI concocted a trumped-up charge of kidnapping and Williams had to flee for his life. He made his way to Cuba, where he was not only granted asylum, but given a press for his paper, *The Crusader,* and a radio station, "Radio Free Dixie," in both of which he advocated armed self-defense as opposed to non-violence. Although not everyone in the civil rights movement agreed with him in 1964, Williams was universally respected and held in high regard.

The questions he raised were becoming of great moment to the movement in those days and his position was one of about four. The polar opposite point of view was held by John Lewis, chairman of SNCC, and Martin Luther King, who had debated Williams at a 1959 NAACP meeting. These two believed passionately in non-violence as a moral imperative and were willing to suffer any consequence rather than personally step into a moral quicksand and countenance violence. Forman and Moses, I would say, saw non-violence as a strategic goal of the Mississippi movement. I doubt they felt non-violence was so much a moral choice as a political one. They felt, correctly, that in the end there was no way of matching arms with the police state, and the black community would suffer much more severe consequences in an eventual shoot-out. Moses did everything he could to see that no arms were kept in the freedom houses or offices that summer. McLaurin and others maybe held a third position that saw non-violence as a useful tactic for the here and now and a good public relations stance, but it seemed to Mac only common sense to have a gun in his car and house, and he had no objection to others doing the same.

But to organize armed self-defense groups would have taken the movement at best into a defensive posture when the crying need was to go on the offensive in Mississippi. The tremendous success we had in Indianola in the face of the armed police state demonstrated that a big mass movement involving unarmed citizens could succeed. But late at night if your home was attacked by nightriders, it made sense to shoot back. As far as I know in the year I was in Sunflower County nobody had ever fired at a nightrider even in self-defense, but weapons were displayed so that the KKK was aware of that possibility. In at least two other counties, however, there had been an exchange of fire. That summer black citizens in the COFO campaign in other parts of Mississippi had already traded fire with KKK types. In McComb a KKK pickup truck on a raid through the black community ended up riddled with bullets, the sheriff said; the nightriders were not injured, or so they pretended. The incident seemed to have had a salutary effect there. In Sunflower County many black citizens kept arms in their houses, but other than that the Freedom Schools and our office in Indianola were weaponless. But in the fall things had to change as the reactionaries became more violent and we needed to have some weapons for defense against night raiders.

In late July the focus of all the projects throughout the state turned to the challenge to the Mississippi delegation at the national nominating convention for president to be held in Atlantic City, New Jersey. In 1964 only a small number of states—California being the most important—chose delegates in primaries; none of these states were in the South. The most common method was to have a state convention, to which delegates were chosen by county conventions, and delegates to those by precinct meetings. (Today the Iowa caucuses retain some semblance of that structure.) The Mississippi Democratic Party excluded blacks from this process; the few registered blacks were almost universally kicked out of precinct meetings if they dared to attend, and the higher-up conventions were all white.

To the end of mounting a credible challenge COFO people tried to enter some of the white precinct meetings only to get tossed out, but more importantly we mimicked the process in the black community on a parallel basis statewide. The Mississippi Freedom Democratic Party held precinct meetings in late July all over the state with large attendance, often much larger than the official white-only meetings. In Sunflower County we had just got going in Indianola and the only precinct meeting was in Ruleville. The county convention was held in early August also in Ruleville, but I think we were able to get some Indianola people to attend it too; maybe Mr. Giles, I don't remember. At any event Fannie Lou

Hamer led the Sunflower delegation to the MFDP state convention and she and McLaurin were elected delegates to the National Democratic Party. A large full, diverse delegation of sixty-eight Mississippi residents (sixty-four blacks and four whites) made up the MFDP delegation; it was headed by Aaron Henry and the co-chair was Ed King, the white chaplain at a private black college in Jackson (Tougaloo) that had been a strong base for the civil rights movement in that city. (After the convention the Ford Foundation threatened that college with starvation of funds unless it stopped supporting civil rights work.) Some older, more conservative NAACP leaders were elected to the delegation, but most delegates were people like Hamer, who had fought for years for equal rights and endured unspeakable atrocities from the hands of the same people who made up the regular Democratic delegation.

In the days before presidential primaries became the norm the state conventions were often the site of so much corruption and various shenanigans that a staple of the national conventions of both parties was deciding which delegation to seat from particular states. There were often two or even more competing delegations from a state. So the Mississippi Freedom Democratic Party challenge was very much part of the custom in 1964. The credentials committee would hold hearings and make a report and the unchallenged delegates would then vote. This process often decided the ultimate presidential candidate, which meant that credential committee hearings were often high drama. (For example, Eisenhower in 1952 was nominated because his challenges of his opponent's delegates won out.)

But President Johnson wanted no drama that year; he expected a unanimous endorsement from the convention, cheering crowds of supporters and no distractions. So he was unhappy with the MFDP challenge. His unhappiness turned to cold fury when Fannie Lou Hamer testified on live television before the credentials committee, eloquently detailing the repression of the state, the denial of the vote to blacks, in particular how she had been kicked off the

Fannie Lou Hamer's televised testimony to the Democratic Party's Credentials Committee riveted the nation and captured its conscience. It was impossible from then on to deny the vicious terrorist police practices of Mississippi, the object of which was to suppress dissent, defy federal law and deny elementary human rights.

plantation for registering to vote, and her own savage beating at the hands of the Mississippi Highway Patrol. With little else to report, since Johnson's nomination was never in doubt, the networks focused on Hamer's testimony and the nation was moved by it. Despite being packed by Johnson's cronies enough of the credentials committee were also moved, if not by Hamer then by the deluge of telegrams that flooded in, so that it seemed very likely that at least a minority report would be submitted to the convention. Big delegations from California, Michigan, New York and Oregon promised that they would support the MFDP over the regular racist delegation in a floor fight, should a minority report get to the floor.

We in Mississippi were riveted to the TV as we watched our David about to slay Goliath. A successful challenge would have capped the summer project with a success unimaginable eight weeks before. Moreover it would be an unmistakable, stinging rebuke to all the state officials, who were nominally Democrats. But behind the scenes President Johnson pulled out all the stops to turn the tide. Jobs, judgeships and federal money were used to bribe and pressure the delegates by the unscrupulous President. Hubert Humphrey, the vice-presidential nominee and formerly loud cheerleader for civil rights, played a particularly pernicious role, lining up the parade of union leaders and moneybags to intimidate the MFDP. Meanwhile Bill Moyers, a top aide to President Johnson, directed a thirty-agent FBI spying and dirty-tricks operation from the White House that targeted SNCC and Martin Luther King in particular. Moyers and his group investigated all the delegates and tried to find some dirt on them, to be used for pressure.[1] After much maneuvering and back and forth, a "compromise" was offered the MFDP: we would get two delegates at large (Fannie Lou Hamer

1. In light of his second career as a great liberal conscience, media critic and general philosopher, Moyers's despicable role in 1964 might seem inexplicable. But in fact he was spymaster for Johnson and this was to continue to be his job for the next three years. He, as a top LBJ aide, had at his beck and call the services of as many FBI agents as needed to find dirt on the President's perceived enemies. He used the FBI in the upcoming campaign against Goldwater and later during the Vietnam War against network reporters who told the unvarnished truth about that war. All this came out after Watergate in testimony to the Senate Investigating Committee.

was specifically excluded as one of them). The regulars had to sign a loyalty pledge to support Johnson, and there would be some kind of reform in four years.

Now immense pressure was put on the MFDP to accept this great largess from the President; the delegation was pressed to accept the "compromise" by a parade of national civil rights leaders, most of whom had not supported the summer project anyway. Martin Luther King, despite immense pressure from Humphrey, was the only one who refused to join the shameful parade; he said little publicly, but told our people that if he were a Mississippi Negro he would reject the compromise. Politicos who had been great verbal supporters of the movement but had done little beyond speechify—like the iconic liberal Senator Wayne Morse, and other people with big connections to liberal money, little of which had gone to Mississippi in recent years in any event—all demanded that that the MFDP accept the "compromise." Even the MFDP's own lawyer, Joseph Rauh, on loan from the United Auto Workers, deserted the delegation and was insistent on caving in. Part of the delegation wavered as Aaron Henry and others were ready to be "realistic." But this was Fannie Lou Hamer's finest hour; she spoke forcefully and any chance that the MFDP would cave was lost after she spoke. She represented the heart of the delegation. Our delegation stood fast for principle and integrity in the face of the corruption and cynicism that so characterized the usual politics in the great democracy. It is very rare that a person so principled, so honest, so completely imbued with a sense of morality like Hamer comes to the fore and is able to gain a place in history. We watching TV in Indianola were so proud of her; Sunflower County was so lucky to count her as a native daughter.

At the convention the regulars balked at signing a loyalty pledge anyway; they were all supporters of Johnson's Republican rival, the arch-conservative, anti–civil rights senator from Arizona, Barry Goldwater. The Mississippi delegation walked out with a handful of other extreme racists from Alabama and South Carolina, so in

The first large demonstration by blacks in Indianola took place on January 4, 1965. Five hundred people picketed the County Courthouse to obtain voting rights and in protest of the flawed election of Congressman Jamie Whitten.

the end nobody represented Mississippi at Johnson's coronation. Some MFDP members got passes from sympathetic delegates and marched to the Mississippi spot, but the chairs had already been removed so they had to stand; a typical white response to blacks who did not know their place. We were to see the same rude tactic used in Indianola when the library was finally desegregated.

But Johnson got what he wanted, a largely unified convention: the moderate racists from the rest of the South stayed in Johnson's camp. Mrs. Hamer was denied a voice at the convention. The President of the USA and leader of the "free world" pushed the civil rights struggle off the TV and gave his acceptance speech to his adoring acolytes. But days before then, disgusted with him and his shenanigans, we in Indianola had already turned off the TV.[2] It was August 29, 1964.

---

2. We in Indianola didn't know even a fraction of the racism and corruption of Humphrey, Johnson *et al.* that was displayed to our delegates by these leaders of the "free world." For example, at a two-hour last-minute negotiation session led by Humphrey, from which Hamer had been explicitly excluded, the MFDP leaders at one point asked for four delegates with two votes so that Hamer and Victoria Grey at least could also be on the floor. Humphrey said: "That is not possible; Fannie Lou Hamer cannot be your delegate." Bob Moses screamed at him: "You are choosing our delegates? You're telling us this is freedom?" Humphrey replied: "President Lyndon Johnson told me that 'illiterate woman must never be allowed to speak again at a Democratic convention, and particularly must not have floor privileges to speak.'" Humphrey went on: "And look at her, the way she dresses, her grammar; this is not the kind of person white America needs to see representing black people." Moses got up to leave and was visibly furious; Humphrey tried to apologize, but Moses slammed the door in his face. (See notes on sources for citation.)

6

The Autumn Desegregation Offensive in Indianola

....

Once more unto the breach, dear friends, once more…
I see you stand like greyhounds in the slips,
Straining upon the start. The game's afoot:
Follow your spirit;

King HENRY V

Just before the convention the bulk of the summer volunteers had left Mississippi for home; the summer project was officially over. Before leaving for Atlantic City McLaurin asked me, John, Charley Scattergood, Gretchen and Linda Davis to stay on for a year; John would head up the project in Mac's absence, since his plan was to enroll in a nearby black college, Mississippi Valley State. By now large numbers of Indianola high school students were hanging around us and they were straining at the slips to do something. It was a given that there would be a boycott of segregated Gentry High in the fall as discussed in the Freedom Schools, and the high school students pretty much on their own, with little or no help from us, had already organized the majority of the thousand or so county black high school students to stay away at least initially.

In the end Gretchen left the project and went back to school and Liz Fusco went to Jackson to direct Freedom Schools for the state. Linda Davis took charge of the Freedom School in Ruleville. John Harris, Charley Scattergood and I then remained in Indianola for the year. McLaurin asked SNCC headquarters that the four of us be accepted as SNCC field secretaries, and soon we were getting those ten-dollar weekly checks from Atlanta. Welcome new blood came to Indianola. Fred Winn, a carpenter who had been in Shaw for the summer came to Indianola and transformed both the Freedom School and the office with his carpentry; he also taught in the Freedom School. A couple, Herschel and Georgianna Kaminsky, came down from Minneapolis and took charge of the Freedom School in Indianola, which became very important given the impending boycott of the regular school. We decided that we needed another car so I went back to Los Angeles at the end of August to get my car, which I had loaned out for the summer.

So before the end of August I caught a ride to New York and then to Rhode Island to see my father, who had some personal problems and had asked for me. I only stayed a few days, but saw my brother who was sympathetic to the movement and to whom I described the summer events. (He was to join the march in Selma, Alabama, later in the year.) Then I got a bus to Los Angeles and spent a couple of days tracking down the irresponsible character to whom I had loaned my car. (He had amassed so many tickets for me to pay that a year later, when I returned to Los Angeles, I was jailed briefly.) In the interim I saw nineteen-year-old Karen Koonan, who had been a frequent visitor to our house in Venice that spring; I had corresponded with her over the summer so it didn't take much to convince her to join us in Indianola as a Freedom School teacher. I drove back to Mississippi after no more than a day or two; Karen followed separately; I probably was away not much more than a week in all.

Karen traveled by a combination of bus and hitchhiking. She met us at the new freedom office and we found her and the

Kaminskys housing in the community as Mrs. Magruder's house was now getting crowded. The Kaminskys were civil rights activists and Karen was also, so the Freedom School soon had a fairly left cast. In addition to its vast collection of black history books and novels by black authors, some radical and pro-Cuba books and pamphlets appeared on the bookshelves, which would have shocked the white press had they been literate enough to notice. The school had students write plays and perform to the community on contemporary life in the Delta. I got on very well with Herschel Kaminsky and we were both on the same page politically; we enjoyed writing descriptive pieces about our project and the political economy of Sunflower County together for fundraising up North.

The school was soon humming with activity as the teenagers planned the big boycott. John, Scattergood and I were not deeply involved in the boycott. I think the students themselves led the effort, guided and helped in no small measure by Herschel and the other Freedom School teachers. Many of the high school kids soon emerged as leaders not only of the boycott, but of all our efforts in the community. The most important new leader was Otis Brown, a seventeen-year-old from a neighboring town in Leflore County. Otis was a bold, intelligent, born leader, who never missed a demonstration or action. He was dynamic in leading activities as well as in planning them carefully. He soon became inseparable from John, Charley and me as we organized for action that month. McKinley Mack from Indianola was another key leader, never afraid and, like me, he loved to laugh at the cops and their cohorts; he was with us in all the action. Some of the other leaders from the high school who worked with us that year in Sunflower and in Indianola were Janell Glass from Moorhead, F.L. Smith, Willie D. Smith, Willie Drain, Steve Mixon, Ronald Strong and Roosevelt Adams all from Sunflower; Riley Rice, Gerald Allen, M.C. Perry, Earl McGhee, Nathaniel Whimbley and Roosevelt Weeks, all of Indianola, and the Taylor sisters, who lived on Senator Eastland's plantation about eight miles out of town. (Taking them home at night was quite an adventure. I had to douse my headlights as we approached the plantation and drive on all sorts of dark dirt tracks to avoid Eastland's armed patrols.) There were probably at least another twenty high school kids who were solid civil rights workers, but I can't remember all the names. New young people were joining the Indianola movement all month, and we had to find housing for some of them as they were being kicked off nearby plantations. A group of about a dozen young black college students led by Bridges Randle would also come to be involved, as well as even a fair number of youngsters of junior high and elementary age, although we tried to keep these younger people from the frontlines. While much education was done at the Freedom School, especially after the boycott was in effect, the Freedom School was also the hub of our organization. In Ruleville Cephus Smith and Ora and Ruby Doss led a contingent of teenagers that, with Linda Davis, became the center of the movement in that town.

In Jackson COFO headquarters provided little or no leadership for a month after the Atlantic City Democratic Party Convention and we were on our own as far as political direction. They did have an all-important WATS telephone line (a precursor to today's 1-800 numbers), which provided a statewide security system and a way to report dangers. Jackson was also the hub for the lawyers from the National Lawyers Guild, whose bold and brave services were indispensable to us. But COFO could provide no money for us so we were on our own for fundraising. The Kaminskys, Linda Davis and some alumni of the summer did a lot of northern fundraising. But our biggest help was Tracy Sugarman, now back in Westport, Connecticut, who virtually organized that progressive artist community into a "friends of Sunflower County" committee. We would come to depend on Tracy for bail money as much as the National Lawyers Guild for legal help.

SNCC and COFO were under heavy attack after Atlantic City from more than just the Mississippi white power structure. President

Johnson was not one to forgive and forget; his attack dogs from the Cold War liberal establishment were soon put in motion and a high-level meeting was held in New York of all civil rights leaders. (Martin Luther King smelled a rat and stayed away.) But the others came, the National Council of Churches, the others who had attacked the Mississippi Freedom Democratic Party in Atlantic City and the NAACP; the meeting was led by one Allard Lowenstein, a collaborator of Hubert Humphrey. Jim Forman, Bob Moses and other top SNCC leaders were touring Africa at the time and just two SNCC workers were invited to hear the edicts from the high priests of civil rights power brokers. They told the hapless SNCC workers of the great dangers of communist infiltration and then issued a set of demands on SNCC to help cleanse their ranks of communists and make SNCC acceptable to liberal democrats. Demand number one: from here on Lowenstein would screen all Mississippi volunteers to weed out the communists (It is likely this guy was some kind of CIA or FBI operative to even assert that authority); number two: the National Lawyers Guild was to be expelled from Mississippi and replaced by the smaller and more timid group of non-communist NAACP and National Council of Churches lawyers; and number three: the Council of Federated Organizations (COFO) would be replaced by some kind of a new NAACP and NCC-controlled organization. Naturally when the SNCC leaders returned from abroad they categorically rejected all of these arrogant demands, and nothing concrete came of all of this except the isolation of SNCC from the established groups (except from King's Southern Christian Leadership Conference). Lowenstein, himself, who occupied some administrative position at Yale spent the fall warning students on that campus not to go to Mississippi to help the civil rights movement because SNCC was infiltrated by communists. Thus for a period much of SNCC's national and statewide energy went into fending off attacks from these kind of liberals.

The crowning irony of this whole dreary affair was that the Communist Party (CP) hated SNCC as much as the Cold War liberals did, as I found out in a most unpleasant meeting in New York about the time the liberals were busy sabotaging SNCC. While waiting in New York for my father to come from Rhode Island to pick me up, I somehow ran into Ron Ridenour, who asked me to join him in a meeting to report on the summer project to the CP Youth group. In a dark office up a rickety elevator in a building in central Manhattan we met a group of about twenty-five not-so-youthful CP'ers, one of whom was Gus Hall, the aging Communist Party leader. We gave an honest account of the summer project, focusing on SNCC's leadership of it and giving little or no credit to the NAACP and others. When we had finished Gus Hall jumped up and launched into a violent and insulting attack on SNCC. He then insisted that the CP's duty was to work with the NAACP and give no support to SNCC, which he considered Chinese influenced. Then his sycophants in the room got up one by one and attacked me and Ron personally; soon, but not soon enough, the awful meeting was over and I was happily on the elevator going down and soon on my way back to Mississippi, telling Ron on the way out to do me a favor and not invite me to any more CP meetings. Ironically the CP was far from even wanting to have anything to do with SNCC; if they were trying to infiltrate anyone, it was the NAACP. But in fact the CP was totally isolated from the civil rights movement and the fear of communist infiltration in SNCC from Johnson's allies was used only to try to weaken SNCC and gain a wedge so that suspicious characters like Lowenstein would replace genuine leaders like Moses, Lewis and Forman.

The SNCC staff, which met after their leaders returned from Africa, was not in the slightest mood to allow Johnson's minions any say in SNCC or the Mississippi Freedom Democratic Party. On the contrary, for some SNCC members the summer project led to major disillusionment with white liberals, not only because of having been stabbed in the back at Atlantic City, but also because in some projects the volunteers had acted in a condescending way to the SNCC veterans. More than a few projects had foundered and fractured as a result of a combination of weak leadership and a poor attitude among the volunteers. On the other hand, successful projects that had strong SNCC leadership like ours in Sunflower County and Lawrence Guyot's in Hattiesburg had made great strides. There was some strong opposition voiced to the proposal of making up to sixty-five of the summer volunteers members of SNCC. Would SNCC be overwhelmed? Would it become a white-run organization like the ones that had sold out in Atlantic City? The stronger and more confident leaders like McLaurin, Guyot and Hamer prevailed, which meant that SNCC expanded and we were accepted. Moses, himself, wanted to step back from leadership given the intensity of the summer, and a number of SNCC veterans decided to go to school in the fall; money was provided by some group for this. All these counter currents led to a period where little general direction was given to the local projects and they all went their own way for about a month. In October Guyot was to make the Freedom Vote a priority statewide and we would soon be all pulling together once more.

In September in Indianola the high school boycott was a tremendous success and the now out-of-school students wanted us to desegregate the city without further delay. We decided to start with the movie theater. Indianola had one movie theater, the only one in the county. The seating system was that blacks had to sit upstairs and whites downstairs; there were separate entrances. Our idea for the evening action was that Scattergood and I would go upstairs, while John Harris, Otis and others would go downstairs. We were neither too secretive nor very subtle about our plans and soon there was a group of about fifty kids who joined us on Church Street, and with this group, much larger than intended, we marched past the courthouse up two blocks into the white section to the movie theater. Before we got there a line of eight or ten police blocked the street to prevent us from reaching our destination. John and I got into an argument with Chief Alexander, who might have changed his mind by now about how John was so easy to get along with.

While the two of us were thus engaged Charles Scattergood and Otis Brown somehow snuck past the cops and were soon buying tickets for precisely the wrong sections, according to the segregation laws. The ticket-seller, aided by some white theater patrons, immediately called this to the cops' attention and the dynamic duo was arrested; Chief Alexander then lost patience with John and, batons at the ready, his cohorts drove us back to Church Street. We were not too deeply disappointed at being so cavalierly deprived of our theater night; nobody even knew what was showing. Instead we were chanting loudly, disturbing the white patrons, and admittedly not being terribly cooperative with the rude police charge, and thus John was quickly arrested; Herschel and I were soon also picked up for failure to obey police orders along with three or four other recalcitrant high school kids; I can't remember exactly who was in this group. Alexander and his minions then drove the remainder of the crowd back to Church Street, while some of us were piled into vehicles destined for the county farm; other arrestees were kept in the Indianola jail. Fred Winn got on the phone to start working on getting our bail money and alerting the lawyers in Jackson.

It was late when we arrived at the county farm and we were ushered into the pitch-black barn where we had been previously incarcerated during the Drew arrests. The two summer months had not diminished the smell of the rat droppings, and in fact there seemed to have been a notable increase in the filth. There were insufficient mattresses so the seven or eight of us spent an uncomfortable and crowded night; Otis, in particular, had some trouble breathing in the foul air. In the morning when we were served the usual fare of coffee, molasses and biscuits we asked the trusty to convey to the captain that we would like mops and brooms to clean the place. This he did, but we didn't think much would come of it. In short order, however, arrived some prisoners carrying mops, buckets and brooms along with the smiling captain, who couldn't believe that the famously lazy civil rights workers would actually want to work.

Elementary schoolchildren were often the most fearless and committed to ending the hated Jim Crow culture. Here, volunteer, Fred Winn, helps make signs. For their own safety we tried, not always successfully, to keep the kids from the main action. A few years later when court cases were finally decided these same children were to be the ones to fearlessly pioneer entrance into the hitherto all-white school system.

But this we did with a vengeance; Hercules worked no less at one of his famous twelve labors. We swept, scrubbed and washed all morning, not only the floors and walls, but also the toilet and wash-basin; trusties carried the buckets full of excrement and dust out of the barn and, before the afternoon "dinner," the surprised captain arrived, inspected the scene and even mumbled a few words that could be taken as complimentary. For dinner, besides the cup of beans and piece of cornbread, he even authorized us to get a slice or two of tomato. That evening we were able to breathe normally and get a good night's sleep on the now sufficient number of mattresses; in the morning we were bailed out, but the work on that barn was well spent since we would soon return.

Unrepentant we decided the next thrust would be on Highway 82. Just north of the Indianola downtown the intersection of highways 49 and 82 gave rise to several small eateries, motels and gas stations. Many of these were local franchises of national chains and, one would think, ready to obey the new Civil Rights Law. So in those late September days we made it a practice to test their compliance. The results were not what one would expect from such a well-advertised law-and-order state. We started with Dairy Queen, dropping off Charley Scattergood a block away, who then walked to the counter and without trouble ordered an ice cream cone for ten cents(!). As he was slowly enjoying the cone, I dropped off Otis and John, who likewise ordered what he was eating; when the new black customers arrived they were told the price was one dollar! Scattergood intervened and insisted that he had only paid ten cents; the flustered owner at first winked and signaled to Scattergood to be quiet, but Charley was only the more loud and firm; so the owner (or franchisee, to be exact) slammed the window shut and said he was closed. We then piled into our car for the Travelodge Motel to book a night's lodging. While waiting at the desk for the clerk to complete a secretive phone call we were none too surprised to see Chief Alexander drive up with some reinforcements and carry us off to the jail. Since there were only four of us we spent the night in the Indianola jail instead of the county farm. With certain variations we repeated the fun during the next two weeks, with the only suspense being whether we get to two or three segregated businesses before Alexander's ragtime band would arrive to arrest us. Sometimes making use of the two cars we would use one car to escape with the bulk of our troops and evade the cops, thus saving hard-to-get bail money.

Naturally this popular activity drew many more volunteers than our overstretched bail fund could afford, so it was decided that John would stay behind to organize the fundraising and legal front. We did try to keep the numbers down in order not to break Tracy and the good people of Westport, but found it hard to deny eager students their right to eat at white-only restaurants. On October 4, however, thirteen of us were arrested at Weber's Restaurant; the cops were getting smarter and they surrounded both cars before we could get away. Besides me, Charley and Otis, two kids from Sunflower, Steve Mixon, Ronald Strong, and eight guys from Indianola (M.C. Perry, Roosevelt Weeks, Charley Taylor, Gerald Allen, Riley Rice, Earl McGhee, Nathaniel Wimbley and Charlie Brown) were among the arrestees. That was too many for the city jail and so it was off to the county farm again. Ronald Strong and I got some extra charges laid on us for being insufficiently cooperative so we were temporarily separated from the rest and interviewed first at the Indianola jail. By some chance an FBI agent arrived while we were there and I demanded to speak to him. While he was desultorily listening to my story and giving body language to indicate how little he cared about civil rights violations, across from us the cops started to interrogate Ron Strong. Ronald had a hat on and to teach him proper respect the Indianola cop without warning gave him a powerful enough blow to the head to make his hat fly off. I shouted to the FBI agent: "Did you see that?" Although the agent was looking right at the cop and Strong he calmly replied to me: "I didn't see anything." The interview with the FBI was over as far as I was concerned. In short order Ronald and I were conveyed to the county farm to join our compatriots in the now relatively clean barn. We were supplied with brooms and mops to spiff up the place, but it was no longer the Augean stables so that job did not take long, and we spent a relatively quiet and comparatively comfortable two or three days before John arrived to bail us out.

In the light of the Ron Strong incident we discussed whether we should be bothered giving reports to the FBI any more. The FBI was highly interested in personal details of the arrestees, but had little interest in what we had to say. They shared the personal information with the local sheriffs, who were free to give it out to their Klan-friendly deputies. The FBI also kept a Washington, DC, database of "troublemakers." On the other hand we could not see anything the FBI presence did to improve our security or that of the local people. John, Charley, Otis and I agreed not to ask for FBI help any more; if they came unbidden we would continue to cooperate, but we kept them at arm's length after October and considered any information given to the FBI as very likely to end up in the hands of the enemies of the civil rights movement. When asked as to our addresses we already were saying "Box 30, Indianola" to protect our hosts, much to the consternation of the cops; the FBI was now told the same.

The county farm, although now clean, was not what you would call comfortable. It had a cement floor, no windows you could look out of (some windows near the roof let in daylight); there was one washbasin and one toilet and no shower. The only furnishings were the mattresses we laid on the floor. But the major advantage was that we were all together, black and white. In the Indianola jail we would always be segregated, Scattergood and I in one cell, John, Otis and whoever else was arrested in the other. If women were arrested they too were separated and kept segregated; women were never sent to the county farm. The biscuits and cornbread at the farm, though in no danger of winning any culinary contests, were a cut above those served at the Indianola jail. In Indianola I would throw pieces of my biscuits out the window onto the adjacent roof to feed the pigeons, but the birds seemed not to find the jailhouse biscuits any more palatable than I. In the jailhouse, there was a bunk, which I made my own, that looked out of the open but barred window onto the roof of an office, which served as the mayor's office and his office for his coal-selling business; beyond that roof you could view a square that led to the library just north of city center. A bunch of pigeons made their domicile near my window, hoping, I suppose, that I would eventually provide better food than those jailhouse biscuits.

In two times in the Indianola jail that September I made the acquaintance of a local white man, the only non-cop white resident of the county I conversed with in my year there. He was a very fat fellow who gave the air of somebody important and this was verified to me when he had his meals brought in from the outside and did not have to eat the jail food. He never, unfortunately, shared a bite with me or Scattergood. He was not particularly friendly to civil rights workers, but we avoided the subject. Scattergood wasn't interested in talking to him, but bored with watching the pigeons on the roof next to the jail I decided to strike up a conversation. He too was bored so we talked; he was in jail for not paying alimony to his former wife, regarding whose purported lack of morality and cleanliness he held forth at some length to me. I said nothing to that, but was cured of any lingering ideas about the vaunted Southern chivalry to women. It appeared that sheriffs could jail one for lack of alimony payments, according to him, if they didn't like the estranged husband. And Sheriff Hollowell most certainly did not like our fellow prisoner, who shared the same feelings toward Hollowell, to whom he referred only in the most lurid language. I, of course, did not care for the sheriff either, so we had that in common, and thus I did not dispute his colorful descriptions of Hollowell's physiognomy or of his alleged habits. He may have been a crop duster, but was, he claimed, an insider in the politics of the county and told me of the tarring and feathering of Hollowell with such detail that I suspected he was in on it. He also told me more of the rivalry between Hollowell and his chief deputy, Parker, as well as the liquor-importing corruption in this "dry" county that they were all part of. He obviously knew we were civil rights workers, but did not say anything about it, nor did I. Well, he was not a fine fellow to be sure, and the conversation was anything but uplifting and erudite; however, he did give one an insight into the thinking that prevailed on the other side of the tracks.

When we got out of the county farm after the Weber's Restaurant arrest John was ready to go for our next project, integrating the county library. Although everyone paid taxes for the library only whites were permitted to use it. Even borrowing books was not allowed for the eighty percent of the people of the county who were black. The library was in a nice building, well furnished and spacious, no doubt largely paid for with federal funds, and only a block from the courthouse. As the school boycott got underway several black students had applied for a library card, but were turned down. They were not handled roughly, just told to please leave by the librarians. In order to draw attention to this injustice we planned a picket line while some students would sit in. There was no dearth of volunteers and on the morning of the picket I was busy ferrying the students from Church Street or Sunflower to the library. Police Chief Alexander and his bosses were hoping to avoid a major arrest at first; they felt particularly vulnerable on the library issue since federal money was used to support the library. To keep the protest in bounds their first step was to arrest me in order to stop the carloads of students from disembarking. I was ushered into the Indianola jail and from my favorite bunk was able to watch the day's events unfold.

The chief's strategy was utterly futile since dozens of kids of all ages made their way on foot to the library, and soon close to a hundred kids were on the picket line while some were inside. The insiders were soon expelled when the library "closed" for the day. The

The black community of Indianola rallies in preparation for Freedom Day. Here Mckinley Mack leads the crowd.

picket line grew too noisy for the cops in the normally tree-lined, quiet, white neighborhood, and in short order Scattergood, Otis and some others joined me in jail. The chief's jackals now lost patience and their discipline broke down. A bus was brought by to arrest all the adults and teenagers. They arrested John and then a woman, who was thrown roughly onto the floor of the bus; John forcefully protested this violence and said, "Don't do that any more." The cop lost all control and John was bashed in the face with a police baton. Now high school kids took the leadership of the picket line as John, his face bleeding, was led to jail. At the jail someone who claimed to be a medic looked at John and said that he would be okay and could go to the county farm without treatment. Meanwhile, one by one the high school–age leaders of the picket line were arrested until only elementary school and younger kids were left on the picket. They were then surrounded and menaced by the big, brave representatives of Indianola's finest, who silenced them and force-marched them around for a while until they ultimately pushed the forty or so little children back into Church Street. Nowadays it is often hard to get kids to use the library; in 1964 it was use the library and go to jail.

We of course by this time had been bussed back to the county farm, while the women remained in the Indianola jail. There were about twenty or twenty-five of us now locked in that barn, and it would be a long wait for the bail money with that many people locked up. First the girls had to be bailed out while we waited for the money to come down from our overtaxed friends up North. We were in there this time for about eight days. John's nose was still bleeding when he got to the county farm. He got no medical attention there; not even a bandage was provided. We used our shirts to fashion makeshift bandages and in a few days the bleeding stopped.

We had no visitors, but on Sunday the captain allowed Fred, Herschel and the others on the outside to bring us sandwiches. However, we had no direct contact with them; the sandwiches were

The library demonstration was way overbooked and initially overwhelmed the police. Little kids went in to ask for library cards while adults picketed. As the police came with a bus to arrest the teenagers and adults, the kids were expelled from the now "closed" library and the police gained control. A long period of incarceration faced the adults as bail funds in the North were depleted. The project subsequently had to redeploy to voter registration. But after the demonstration the library did then allow blacks to use it for the first time, but only after they removed all the seats inside.

By late morning all the adults and teenagers had been arrested leaving only little kids to picket the library. The Police were unable to decide what to do about them, since they were not the least intimidated.

passed to us by means of the trusties. But the sandwiches had notes inside the bread slices telling us what was going on with the bail and encouraging us to hang in there. We had discussions and semi-classes in the day; but the nights were dark and boring. Eventually we were bailed out. In the meantime there was a small victory as the library, for the first time, allowed black people to borrow books and get a library card. However, all the chairs were first removed from the library so that nobody, black or white, could now sit down there, lest a black person might by accident be found sitting next to a white person.

In those September days I stayed with John and Scattergood in Mrs. Magruder's house. Almost every morning it seemed the phone would ring for John and he would at the end of the conversation say to me, "always something." Most of the time the problem was not arson, shootings or the like but all the little problems that can daily bedevil such a diverse project: personality problems among the volunteers for John to mediate, broken mimeograph machine (a hand-cranked type of earlier copier) or car problems—we had many of these with all the driving and the many different drivers. Guy McComb, a black mechanic in Indianola, became indispensable to us and always gave us a good rate and fast service.

With such a large contingent of civil rights workers who were out-of-school high school kids from the town of Sunflower, I made many trips up there in that period to give them rides to Indianola, and thus got to know the tiny town and its people. It was a very small town, smaller than Ruleville, about eight miles up Highway 49 from Indianola, and was very impoverished, even by Ruleville or Drew standards. Chief Deputy Parker ran the town as his own bailiwick. Sunflower also had a daytime policeman, Speedy Miles and a small jail, and Miles could count on a part-time night cop, a short, slender half-wit named Willy Wood. In better times Saturday nights had seen the town humming as many hundreds of plantation workers streamed in to let off steam. But now almost all the stores were boarded up and few people came even on the weekends. The houses were almost all tiny but neat and clean and wooden and often had a little vegetable garden and chicken coop in the back. I never saw the white section, but it had just a few dozen houses. The black section with a hundred houses covered four streets to the highway and each street stretched for about four or five blocks. The church was located near the highway. There was a small grocery store, poorly stocked and dusty, and that was about it. The population was over ninety percent black.

The one nice, modern house in the black community with a big picture window was located across from the jail and abutted the street, which had once been the main drag (today in 2013 all the shops are boarded up). It belonged to Annie Mae King, the mother of Ronald Strong, and a former cook in the white school; she was very welcoming to me from my first visit to the town. She had gone down to register to vote earlier, having heard about the Ruleville people, after which she was promptly fired from her job. She would often feed me and introduce me to the other black adults in town. The church was also welcoming and the pastor happened to be Rev. Kirkland, the same man who had given us use of the Freedom School in Indianola. He initially did not want us to hold meetings in the Sunflower church, but we were welcome to speak during services and he often sermonized on our behalf without being asked. I started attending services, at first to speak, but since the custom was that one of the ladies of the church would hold a sumptuous feast for Rev. Kirkland after services, I learned to hang out with him after church, and he would then invariably invite me to Sunday dinner, by far my best meal of the week. There was potato salad, chicken, many types of greens and beans—more than I could eat, which was a lot. So I tended to spend more and more time in Sunflower in September and early October.

Ronald Strong was not part of the library bust for some reason. But Miles, the Sunflower cop, picked him up anyway while we were in the county farm and jailed him. Ronald had reason to believe the cops intended to use him badly and he feared for his life. None of our people in Indianola knew of his arrest and neither did we in the county farm; hence he was isolated and very vulnerable. That night Ronald, who was as strong as his name, made a hole in the roof of the jail and escaped. He kept going until he reached Chicago and stayed there with relatives. Mrs. King was furious at his treatment by Parker's minions and at the same time desolate at her loss. He was her only companion in her house. When I got out of the farm I went to see her and asked about Ronald. She told me the story and then totally, to my surprise, said she was going to Washington to live with her sister for a while. She gave me the keys to her house and said I should use it as a freedom office in Sunflower, and could stay there as long as I liked.

I talked it over with John and we decided I should move out of Mrs. Magruder's house in Indianola to Sunflower. For safety's sake I would keep the car there and at least one high school student would always room with me. Initially Earnest Smith, who had been kicked off some plantation for working with us, moved in. But often the people there varied from night to night. Parker and his good old boys wasted no time in threatening me, making night-time forays in front of the house and causing some minor vandalism at the house. But the house was humming in the day with two dozen or so of the local kids; at night we had three or four huge, industrial-grade fire extinguishers and a rifle to keep us company. These would soon come in handy. This was around October 15, 1964.

7

The Klan Strikes Back

....

Mischief thou art afoot;
Take thou what course thou wilt.
Cry "Havoc" and let slip the dogs of war

Julius CAESAR

For the first time in years early September saw crosses being burned in Sunflower County. This was the sign that the Ku Klux Klan was organizing in the county and ready to take action against us. For a decade the White Citizens' Council had the monopoly on repression with its combination of police methods, economic reprisals and some measure of nightriding intimidation. But a large portion of the white population now grew impatient with these mild prescriptions and the murder, mayhem and arson promised by the Klan were becoming popular. There were several reasons for this:

- The breakthroughs in Indianola and Sunflower showed we were expanding and the White Citizens' Council was powerless to stop us.
- The summer project, which they thought they could wait out, now showed no sign of ever ending.

- The desegregation efforts in Indianola showed we were not at all afraid of challenging the core practices to their "way of life."
- The high school boycott showed that we had a broad base of support from young people, just as the mass meetings had demonstrated the same among people of all ages.
- Cracks and fissures appeared among law officers and petty officials with many of the younger ones much more inclined to the action program of the KKK.
- A school desegregation case was moving through federal court and soon at least one school system in the county would be integrated.

Under the benevolent protection of the powerful Parker in Sunflower the Klan seemed to have recruited the largest number of operatives in the county from around that town. Their goal was to drive us out of Sunflower, burn down the Freedom School in Indianola and take action against black families and churches that were part of the movement in both towns. The cross-burning, white hoods and silly rituals were as much directed toward impressing the ignoramuses that wanted to join the KKK as they were an intimidation factor to the local community.

We had plenty of intelligence as to what was afoot, and more to make a point than anything else John and I went to the Indianola gun shop and asked to buy some rifles. We were turned down on some excuse or other, which we expected, and then we went twenty miles to the neighboring town of Greenville, where we made the purchase with ease. The sheriff was upset at the attempted purchase. He called John and me aside and made a point of telling us he knew of the attempt; we referred to the many threats, but did not tell him of our purchase in Greenville, of which he was ignorant. I took one gun to Sunflower, John kept one in Mrs. Magruder's house and usually one was kept in the freedom office in Indianola. At the same time our donors in the North were asked to provide industrial-grade fire extinguishers, which we kept in the places where we slept and in the Freedom School.

In October there were three separate attacks on Mrs. King's house in Sunflower, where I slept. This house was easy pickings for the Klan trainees since it was on a large lot on the main dirt road in the black section, yet very close to the city jail and within two blocks of the safety of the white section. Nevertheless the initial attacks had little success and the worst was a fire started around the foundation of the house and around my car. I easily put it out with the fire extinguishers and when the deputies arrived, supposedly to help even though we had never called them, I had a rifle cradled in my arm more for show than anything else. The scene was straight out of the movies as the deputies arrived; I can remember it in some detail; I held a rifle in one hand, a flashlight in the other; Earnest Smith, who was only fourteen, had the fire extinguishers and was putting out a few lingering hot spots. The scene couldn't have been better if it had been staged; well, it was staged to some extent. The look on the deputies' faces was precious; someone must have told them we were non-violent. I only wished John could have seen it in person instead of relying on my description the next day. Of course, had I actually had to use the rifle it would not have been a successful moment. In my one semester of college Reserve Officers' Training (ROTC) I had placed dead last out of two hundred in marksmanship class.

This show of force on our part forced a change in KKK tactics and a few days later, on October 28, they lobbed a military-grade tear gas canister through the plate glass window—the investigating FBI agent later opined it came from a National Guard armory. We were woken up immediately, but within seconds the house was so filled with gas that each of us was trapped in our separate bedrooms. I managed to get my window open and got out, but Earnest panicked and I couldn't get him to unlock and open the window so I smashed it open with the rifle butt and he climbed out, but not before he got a major gash on his knee from the jagged glass. I drove to Indianola with Earnest and got John and we went to the Freedom School to get a first-aid kit, since Earnest was now bleeding copiously. When we got there a fire had been set inside the library and we had to put it out with the fire extinguishers, which we kept there. That took about fifteen minutes and delayed our being able to treat Earnest, whom we had left at Mrs. Magruder's house. But with makeshift bandages Mrs. Magruder was able to staunch the bleeding. When John and I came back with the first-aid kit we applied more bandages, but thought it best to take him to a hospital in a city where we were unknown. We drove to Greenville and John, posing as his brother, got him stitched up. He required sixteen stitches. The damage to the Freedom School was not major and only required some expert carpentry from Fred and some more donations of books.

But the people of Indianola were incensed at this attack on their Freedom School and rallied the next day outside the school. The cops swinging clubs broke up the demonstration. We were able to get a glazier from Greenville to replace the picture window in Mrs. King's house and the glass in the bedroom. Meanwhile at Sunflower, F.L. Smith organized a group of nine young men to guard the house to prevent break-ins by Parker's minions. Willy Wood came by on October 29 and threatened to kill them. When I went back to staying there the next night, two other Sunflower kids, Willie Drain and Willie D. Smith, volunteered to stay with me and we went on as before.

In those days the national press, so ubiquitous in July, was completely invisible. The story of Mississippi had lost its spot on the evening news and nothing of all these events ever made the television or newspapers, even though we sent out press releases. Instead the focus of the press was now on the monumental battle for the presidency between Johnson and Goldwater, and our little troubles in the Mississippi Delta could not compete for front-page or even back-page attention. The center of Johnson's Mississippi effort was focused on the town of Greenville on Highway 82, only twenty-four miles from Indianola.

Greenville, located on the Mississippi, was quite an anomaly for the state; it was perhaps the only town controlled neither by the White Citizens' Council nor the KKK. The Hodding Carter family, who were the only white politicians and publicists of note in the state to support President Johnson, controlled the politics of the town. Their daily, *The Greenville Press-Democrat,* had never joined the insane frenzy about the summer "invasion" and seemed quite content that Johnson's strategy of keeping the Mississippi Freedom Democratic Party at bay was good enough to keep the status quo. Therefore violence and intimidation were of no utility and just unnecessarily threatened business, since the Carter family believed that the civil rights movement would pose no danger to any change of life in the Delta for some time to come. This town, unlike the rest of the Delta, was not in decline and was happy to go its own way. We found it much easier to do business in Greenville, whether to buy food, get repair people or to use the hospital. The level of nastiness to black people was at a discernibly lower level in that town. More and more blacks from Indianola who had transport also would go to Greenville to avoid being called "boy" or "girl," when they bought their groceries, which was the insulting custom in the Indianola Piggly-Wiggly. Hodding Carter, who was later to occupy a major position in Jimmy Carter's administration—they were not related—was a segregationist to be sure, but he was a rare voice in not supporting violence. Since the regular Democrats put Goldwater on their Mississippi ballot, the Johnson people relied on Hodding Carter to field a slate for the President. The Mississippi Freedom Democratic Party had already offered to field a slate for Johnson but Johnson wanted nothing to do with us so Carter was his man. With no minor difficulty Carter was able to get Lyndon Johnson, a sitting President, on the Mississippi ballot; the road-blocks Mississippi placed in his way were an indication of the ter-rorist state's fear of a contested election, even when blacks were disenfranchised. But by means of that maneuver the MFDP would now be denied a place on the official ballot.

Despite the snub the MFDP decided that we would run Johnson and Humphrey as our presidential candidates along with Aaron Henry for US senator and, in our district, Fannie Lou Hamer as candidate for Congress. This smart strategic decision did not go over really well with some SNCC people, who rightly harbored ill feelings toward LBJ. Lawrence Guyot, who chaired the Mississippi Freedom Democratic Party, caught no small amount of flak from his fellow SNCC workers. But Guyot was a brilliant student of politics and realized that our putting up posters for Johnson alongside those of Hamer and Henry was striking a blow against the state and empowering our movement. Guyot fought for MFDP's independence from SNCC and maintained that the MFDP was its own organization and in any event did not need SNCC's permission for its political decisions. So in Giles's Grocery Store, the White Rose Café and in many other black businesses and some homes one saw in the window the square-foot posters of Johnson, Humphrey, Hamer and Henry side by side. When it came to putting up bumper stickers or wearing buttons we tended to put just Hamer up.

Lawrence Guyot was one of the first Mississippians to join SNCC and he in fact had recruited Charles McLaurin. He was a very large man with huge arms and when he spoke he gesticulated vigorously, one could say almost wildly, with them. I once had the misfortune of being seated during a SNCC meeting directly in front of him and when he got up to speak I feared being banged on the head with his gestures. He was neither a model of brevity nor of soft-spokenness like Bob Moses and though I normally hung on Guyot's every word, since his political analyses were so keen, at that meeting I could not concentrate on what he was saying so sure I was that my head was about to be dealt a serious blow.

Both Bob Moses and Dave Dennis were withdrawing from leadership that fall, and new people and volunteers kept the office in Jackson functioning. Everyone had always looked to Moses for leadership, but he felt the weight of events that summer too much and did not want that role any more. He even announced he changed his name to Parris, since he never liked the comparison with the biblical Moses, which Fannie Lou Hamer often made in her singing. So with the Council of Federated Organizations now functioning more as a coordinating center Guyot and the Mississippi Freedom Democratic Party provided the political direction to the projects. Guyot's leadership that fall was critical to giving statewide direction to our movement.

The MFDP plan was to hold a "freedom vote" to parallel the regular election. We would hold our own registration procedures and follow with freedom votes close to election night. Given the difficulties, we were allowed a little leeway and started collecting ballots a few days early. Since Hodding Carter's pro-Johnson campaign was invisible, at least in Sunflower County, the only real contest was between the MFDP's freedom vote and the state-sanctioned vote for Goldwater, the Republican from Arizona. Goldwater presented himself as a man of intellect and principle, but once this false veneer was scratched what really appeared was a reckless warmonger, a foolish isolationist and rustic, a fierce opponent of civil rights, and one so backward in his politics that he wanted to scuttle all the New Deal programs like Social Security, and bring back the America of 1932. Johnson, as unlikable and corrupt as he was, looked better and better to most Americans by comparison as the campaign wore on.

The Mississippi Freedom Democratic Party had been founded at a COFO meeting in the spring of 1964. Originally the idea was to use it as a vehicle to challenge the regular Democrats. If this had worked then there would not have been a need for the MFDP; we would have all been Democrats and the putative Democrats like Eastland would have been Republicans and have lost their seniority in Congress. But the MFDP was blocked and stymied in such a way that a big majority in the MFDP didn't want to give up their independent organization for the corruption of the national Democratic Party. Guyot, who was in jail during the Atlantic City Convention, was a strong proponent of keeping the MFDP independent and viable. He worked hard with the help of Hamer and others to make it a force in the state and a strong organization. It was in this context that the MFDP endorsed Johnson-Humphrey and ran the freedom vote.

In the second congressional district our ballot allowed the freedom voters to choose Hamer or Whitten for Congress (there were two other districts where MFDP had different congressional candidates). Also there was Henry vs. Eastland for senator and Johnson vs. Goldwater for president. We spread out to wider and wider areas of the county in late October as we campaigned, put up posters and registered freedom voters. For the vast number of black people this was the first real exercise in democracy and many people got involved. It took some courage to display a bumper sticker or put up a poster even of President Johnson in those days. In Sunflower an older brother of F.L. Smith put a Hamer bumper sticker on his car and found the car stolen and torched a few days later. Despite all of this we wanted Rev. Kirkland to allow the Sunflower church to be used for the collection of freedom vote ballots in Sunflower. Generally for security reasons we only collected ballots in daylight, but still, with good reason, Kirkland feared for his church.

Oscar Giles and other leading deacons, like Mose Griffin, wanted very much to support our efforts. There was no person more personally supportive of me in Sunflower than Oscar Giles. A kindly, but morally strong man in his late thirties or early forties, he owned a small farm near Sunflower and with his wife ran the Giles Penny Saver Grocery Store in Indianola. He worked hard but was independent. He was universally respected in the town and in the church; I found his advice and counsel essential. I would go out to his farm very often and more often than not stay for dinner. His and his wife Alice's hospitality was always incredibly warm and inviting. They had a small daughter, whom I would bounce on my knee, New England style. There was no other home I felt so much a part of that year. One time I even got stuck in the mud and he got his tractor to pull me out. I raised with him the idea that we

Oscar Giles and his wife Alice were independent farmers and grocery store owners. Giles was a founding member of the Sunflower County NAACP in 1954 and a registered voter, who survived the ten-year fierce state repression of that organization. He rallied the black community of Sunflower in 1964 to give warm and unstinting support to the movement and to open up its church to the Civil Rights workers.

needed a precinct to collect ballots to give legitimacy to our freedom vote. He understood the dangers but readily agreed and within a day the church approved. Now we had precincts, not only in Ruleville like in 1963, but also in Indianola and Sunflower. This would be a major step forward in increasing participation.

The town of Moorhead was now canvassed for the first time, largely by Charles Scattergood, Janell Glass who lived there, and some other high school kids from Indianola. There was clearly interest in that town and John and I joined them one morning. The question of finding a building for the precinct in that town that day seemed very important to our expanding to that fourth town. Janell had a suggestion of a vacant structure, and she was sure the owner would agree. Unfortunately the woman who owned the building was away for a few weeks staying with relatives in the tiny hamlet of Tippo, located in Tallahatchie County, north and east of Ruleville. There was just one road in and out of Tippo.

So without thinking too much about any dangers, John and I left Moorhead around noon for Ruleville and drove east on Highway 8 for about twenty miles. There at a tiny settlement called Phillipp we left the paved road for a one-lane dirt track with cotton fields on both sides which led to Tippo in about twenty miles. There was not another vehicle on that road. In about five miles we passed a road grader off the dirt road parked in the field with a white driver who watched us. Something about that did not seem right to us so John started fiddling with our two-way radio in the SNCC car, just randomly moving the tuner dial, while I drove. After a minute or two of just static we heard the following conversation: "Where are they?" "About ten miles from Tippo. There's a nigger and a nigger-lover." "What's the car look like?" "It is a white Plymouth." "Well, by the time it gets to Tippo it will be red with their blood."

I looked at John and he looked at me and without missing a second I wheeled the car around and at top speed raced back down the dirt road. In five miles the road grader was now moved off the field and stood in the middle of the road blocking our way. Without slowing down very much I turned into the cotton field around the road grader and after mowing down some cotton plants I was back on the road. Without losing any speed I turned right on the paved road, pushed the speed up to close to a hundred miles an hour and we didn't stop till we reached Ruleville. There, at the Freedom School, we stopped to catch our breath in the late afternoon and ran into McLaurin, to whom we told the story. He smiled, shook his head and said he personally never went to Tallahatchie County; it was too dangerous. That county was where Emmet Till had been murdered not six years before. We gave up the idea of a precinct in Moorhead and instead, when the time came, Charles Scattergood and Janell Glass collected the ballots and deposited them in the Indianola precinct, not strictly by the rules, but who could blame us?

That citizens' band or CB radio, which we had rarely used up till now, seemed to have saved our lives. In the wake of the lynching of Chaney, Schwerner and Goodman a northern group raised money to put CB two-way radios in each SNCC car. The idea was that if a lynching party approached we could then communicate our whereabouts. These radios were much less handy than the modern cell phones. The problem was that these radios could not call a telephone number only another CB radio and there had to be an operator on standby tuned to the same frequency as the transmitter to get the calls. They also had a short range, about thirty miles, so each project would have to have someone monitoring calls. This was not practical so in effect the well-meaning CB radio idea fell into disuse quickly. But what we could do was listen in to calls other people made in the area we were in. Usually only deputies and truckers used these devices so we could listen in to their conversations just by turning the dial until you heard something of interest. We rarely did this, but something about that long road to Tippo made us suspicious so John was just randomly turning the dial when he heard the enemy set up an ambush. We must have been spotted at Phillipp and then by the road grader so they had to communicate by CB to alert their cohorts in Tippo to be ready for us. It was this conversation that we luckily happened upon.

The freedom vote went very well in Sunflower County; our numbers were vastly up from 1963. This was not the case in most other counties. In Indianola and Sunflower the freedom vote exceeded the vote collected at the official white-only precincts. The fact that so many masses of blacks were actively participating was very disconcerting to the white power structure and the Klan saw that its intimidation was not working. Crosses were being burned with increasing frequency in the days before the election, with no effect on us or on the freedom voters. But every indication was for us to expect more than burning crosses on election night. The Klan made no secret that there would be serious arson on election night. The black maids reported to us from conversations they had overheard that serious preparations for violence in white households were underway. The whites in Mississippi actually expected that

Goldwater would win the election and therefore they could kill and burn once again with impunity.

In fact the election was to be a landslide victory for Johnson who, with sixty-one percent of the popular vote, had the biggest presidential victory ever. To paraphrase Dr. Samuel Johnson in an earlier time about a long-forgotten other scoundrel, Goldwater's last refuge was racism. He only carried the states where blacks were excluded in large numbers from voting: Mississippi, Louisiana, Alabama, Georgia and South Carolina (he squeaked by in his native Arizona). In Mississippi Goldwater won by eighty-seven percent, so no wonder all the whites thought he was going to win since everyone to whom they talked had voted for the racist slate. Johnson, never one to forgive and forget, particularly targeted the Goldwater states in the Voting Rights Bill, which he muscled through Congress the next year.

We anticipated both the national and state results, but as election day approached the problem of protecting our precincts assumed great importance. The Freedom Schools in Indianola and Ruleville were targets and, as always, the house I lived in was a major bone sticking in the local Klan's throat. But my biggest worry was the Sunflower church, made of wood, which was on a corner three blocks from where I stayed and only one block from the highway; it would be a fairly easy target for nightriders. We had used the church against Rev. Kirkland's better judgment and I felt a special obligation to protect it. I discussed the matter with Oscar Giles and Mose Griffin and they both agreed that we needed to defend the church. Some deacons and members of the church provided guns to me and there were plenty of volunteers among the youth to help.

Our best guess was that Annie Mae King's house was the prime target so the largest force would stay with me in her house. About ten to fifteen young men—in those still sexist times the young high school women were sent home—came to stay with me; a number of them were armed. The house and yard were well lit and we had patrols in front. Roosevelt Adams, who was seventeen, and another guy the same age, both of whose judgment I trusted and respected, went to the church. They took the rifles donated by the church deacons and the church was purposely kept dark. Unknown to me an older guy, maybe twenty-two years old, who was visiting his old hometown but now lived in Chicago, joined them. At around eight in the evening John drove up from Indianola to collect the ballots and go over the security arrangements with me. He kept the car that night since they were also patrolling Indianola and the Freedom School there.

Not long after John left, Willy Wood, the night cop from Sunflower, was at the church with a flashlight and a gun and it looked to the guys inside that he was about to set a fire near the foundation. The visitor from Chicago grabbed a rifle ran out of the church and aimed the rifle directly at Willy, saying "Willy, watch yourself die." He pulled the trigger but something went wrong and the rifle just clicked. Willy fled. The Chicagoan dropped the rifle and fled; we never saw him again. Adams and his friend bravely went back into the church to resume their post. But Willy alerted the other deputies and within minutes twenty of them surrounded the church; they must have been waiting. From where we were in Mrs. King's house we couldn't see the church, but we couldn't miss the carloads of deputies and other thugs racing for the church. Some young black guys from the town then came up to our house and told us that the church was surrounded and Adams was refusing to surrender. Leaving four or so guys behind to keep the house guarded, the rest of us marched to the church some three blocks away. There were at least twenty-five young men with me; some had pistols, but I was unarmed.

We stopped about twenty yards from the church and faced the armed deputies/klansmen. Although they were better armed than my group they were not necessarily in a good tactical position, caught between two groups of armed young black men, and they knew it. Deputy Parker was in charge of his group but he clearly didn't know what to do. I also could see a potential disaster in the making so I approached the deputies alone and Parker and I separated from our groups and privately negotiated. I wanted to get the kids safely out of the church and my group safely back to Mrs. King's house. Parker was clearly worried about his skin and that of his friends if there was a shoot-out, but he told me he needed to arrest the kids in the church, since they tried to kill Willy. I told him I had given them the guns and was responsible, and I didn't want the kids arrested. I proposed a compromise, which he readily accepted. Roosevelt and his friend would leave the rifles behind and come out and join my group; they would then all go to Mrs. King's house and the deputies would go home. Once these conditions were met I would stay behind and Parker could arrest me on whatever charges he wanted.

We both fulfilled our ends of the bargain: I went into the church and got the kids out and escorted them through the deputies to the large group of kids a few yards away; the kids were safe and together. The deputies, if that's what they were, went home. I signaled to the kids to leave; they were reluctant to leave me alone, but I insisted. I then got into Parker's car for a destination unknown. Neither the church nor Mrs. King's house was bothered that night. The kids continued their vigil at the house but all of them ended up safe; there were no further arson attempts at the church. I ended up in the Indianola jail; the white cell was empty so I had the cell to myself. Upon my arrest somebody from Sunflower borrowed a car and drove to Indianola and told John what had happened. (Remember, there were no phones available to us.) John made it known to the sheriff that he expected me to be safely handled. The next morning John arrived with sandwiches and chicken and a book Herschel picked out for me: James Joyce's *Portrait of the Artist as a Young Man*. I finished the book in jail, while for a few days the community of Indianola sent me lots of food. It took our lawyers a few days to figure this one out. They met with Sheriff Hollowell and worked out a deal. Parker or Hollowell decided to forget about the threat to kill Willy, since it was just the latter's word and the Chicagoan was long gone. (There had been some bitter previous history between the two, I gathered, which nobody wanted to come out.) Since the whole incident was generally embarrassing to all concerned, this time there would be no bail or removal of the case to federal court; it would be settled quickly and quietly. I was to plead guilty to giving guns to a minor and pay a one-hundred-dollar fine.

The lawyer explained this all to me on Friday and I followed the script. While we were waiting for the justice of the peace to finalize the deal, Hollowell spent the time telling the lawyer how much he wanted me to go back to UCLA and get on with my studies. The lawyer politely listened and I kept quiet during this monologue. The main idea that was emphasized was to keep the whole incident secret and then SNCC wouldn't be taxed about not being non-violent, while the deputies would not be made to look as if they had been forced to back down to a bunch of black kids. We said nothing, but Parker, or more likely some of his friends, spilled the beans. The next issue of the *Indianola Enterprise-Tocsin* had as its main story: the COFO worker who was arming young blacks. Fearing that this might not sit well at our Jackson headquarters, John and I met with McLaurin to explain the situation. He was most supportive and said that of course we had done the right thing. He said that he himself had spent election night armed and guarding the Freedom School in Ruleville. He would squelch any possible complaints from SNCC. There were none that we heard of.

When I went with Parker in his car that night I had no guarantee that I would not be shot and left on the side of the road, à la James Chaney. I didn't know the kids would look out for me to the extent they did by finding someone with a car to drive to Indianola to alert John. My trepidations on that ride were compounded when the driver took some back road that I didn't recognize. One can imagine my relief when after a period of silence Parker turned to me and said, "I guess after Goldwater wins this election you scalawags (or some such phrase) are going to be all hightailing it out of Mississippi." Up until that moment I wasn't assured of having that option. However, instead of expressing gratitude I told him Goldwater had no chance of winning and would only carry Mississippi and Alabama. I then went on to say that we were staying no matter what and was about to continue talking along that line; I stopped, thinking of my precarious position, and finally shut up. Parker was not a debating man and said nothing further. Shortly afterwards I was very glad to see the not-so-bright lights of Indianola and to be delivered to my cell. I flopped down on my favorite bunk, and quickly fell asleep. It was November 3, 1964.

8

A Winter to Keep On Pushing

....

Thus sometimes hath the brightest day a cloud;
And after summer evermore succeeds
Barren winter with its wrathful nipping cold:
So cares and joys abound as seasons fleet.

HENRY VI Part II

A popular song of that year was called "Keep on Pushing." SNCC people tended to adopt it as a supplementary anthem to "We Shall Overcome." Typically Mrs. Hamer changed it to "Keep on keeping on," to emphasize the long hard struggle with so few results. The original song had the line, "Keep on pushing, move up a little higher." So "Keep on keeping on" seemed more in tune with the reality of that year in Mississippi.

We didn't hear from the KKK for nearly two months after the election night incident. Basically they always had been a cowardly lot, founded by two incompetent generals of the treasonous army in 1865 and manned locally by the dregs of that disbanded Confederate Army, the ones who had avoided direct combat in the war; the ranks were filled as well with illegal whiskey distillers, sadists, rapists and the worst type of common criminals. The KKK never challenged the occupying Union Army and hid their identities behind hooded sheets, doing their dirty work at night. They normally attacked isolated farms owned by blacks or whites who cooperated with the Reconstruction; even then, not taking any chances, they came in groups of fifty or more to attack single families. Arson, tarring and feathering and murder were the specialties of these craven thugs, but they never put themselves at risk. They were suppressed by President Grant in 1872, although after his term the Supreme Court issued a series of rulings to protect the rights of lynchers and arsonists from federal legislation, and as a result violence against blacks got inexorably and steadily worse in the late nineteenth and early twentieth century. The Klan was reborn with great fanfare in 1915 after the appearance of a racist film, *Birth of a Nation* by D. W. Griffith, glorifying the Klan; the film was endorsed by President Woodrow Wilson, who had made little secret of his personal sympathy for the Klan in his previous career as a history professor. Much of the Klan's modern regalia and traditions, including cross-burnings, were invented by the filmmakers with help from Woodrow Wilson's spurious history books. Some six million whites in the country eventually became members by 1924, most of them just attracted by the stupid parades and weird traditions, exactly as many Germans were attracted at that very same time to the Nazis for similar reasons. But the violent core of this depraved group now organized thousands of the same cowardly lynchings against isolated blacks, which had been a Southern custom over the past sixty years.

The modern KKK of the fifties and sixties, now much smaller, carried on this inglorious tradition; it took twenty-five of them to lynch the unarmed Chaney, Schwerner and Goodman. So the show of arms by two teenagers on election night in the Sunflower church made them stay away from there for the better part of a year, even though we did not actively guard it any more. They likewise left me alone in Annie Mae King's house for a while, which meant we could concentrate on our work.

Now that the election was over the Mississippi Freedom Democratic Party decided it would challenge the seating of the

Mississippi "elected" representatives, with a view to having Fannie Lou Hamer, Victoria Gray and Annie Devine seated in their place. The new Congress would open in January and at least some House members said they would support the challenge. The hope was the racist delegation would not be sworn in and then hearings would be held to see if the MFDP slate or the segregationists should represent the three Mississippi districts that were in dispute. Guyot coordinated this effort in Washington. Our job in the field was to collect depositions and line up witnesses to back up the fact that the official slate was chosen in rigged elections where the majority had been disenfranchised. So our daily work involved getting statements and potential witnesses, the best of which would be formally deposed by lawyers, with even a few flown to Washington, DC. I walked every block of black Sunflower and knocked on every door. Almost everyone gave me some kind of statement. On Sundays I talked at the church and explained what we were doing. In all of this, of course, the kids accompanied me and helped. They went to places I couldn't go like Senator Eastland's plantation and got statements from people out there.

On Mondays I would go to Indianola and get my ten-dollar check. John, Scattergood and I would then go to the White Rose Café and buy some hamburgers and drink a pint of scotch with some local friends. On Saturday nights we went to Club Ebony, where B.B. King would sometimes sing. When he did, he always bought the civil rights workers a big meal. If he wasn't there someone else would often buy us a chicken dinner, or the owner, B.B. King's adoptive mother, would serve us and never charge. On Sundays after church I was always invited to the dinner given to the pastor and usually it was quite a feast. Sometimes for lunch Mrs. Smith would cook a big pot of collard greens for me and her son and nephew. On other days I just bought a loaf of bread, some bologna and got some cabbage in place of lettuce from the garden Mrs. King's brother kept going even in the winter. If I was in Indianola, Mrs. Magruder would cook for us or if there was money we ate at the White Rose Café. I got by and didn't starve. And when the winter got cold since there was no heat in the house I just piled on about ten quilts and warmed up that way. How, or even if, I did my laundry I don't remember; probably some lady in the community came over and did it for me without saying anything when the smell got too bad.

In Sunflower my closest companions were F.L. Smith and Janell Glass. F.L. was the youngest of seventeen children raised by the gregarious and kindly Mrs. Smith, who was the lady in town who looked after me the most. F.L. was a tall fellow; at twenty years old he was older by two or three years than the other youths; he was fairly mature for his age and a very keen observer. F.L. was highly articulate and had a great sense of humor, with a sardonic wit that kept me always entertained; he in turn was always asking me questions about history and politics. We enjoyed each other's company immensely. We had an organization called the "Sunflower Youth Movement," of which he was president. Janell might have been the vice-president; she was a personable and highly intelligent young woman from Moorhead who had a one-year-old daughter, but she spent most of her time that winter in Sunflower with us while her mother watched the child. She was an indefatigable canvasser who seemed to know everyone in that part of the county. Also at the "freedom house" on most days were Willie D. Smith—F.L.'s nephew—the Taylor sisters from Eastland's plantation, Roosevelt Adams and Steve Mixon. Steve was brave, had a bright sense of humor and was always smiling, no matter what the situation. Despite the miserable formal education these kids had they were very astute politically and full of wide-ranging questions and observations. So we normally had quite a group during the day when we were canvassing or just having discussions. We sometimes would break for lunch and the kids delighted in introducing me to what was new food for me like pig feet and ears and chitterling. At night at least two of the young men would stay with me. In the afternoons normally a dozen or more local kids would hang out with me at the house. We had no television or even a radio so we talked. Conversations ranged from mundane gossip to national politics and international developments. The kids were all fantastically engaged and we all learned a lot from each other while having a good time.

One day in late fall we got word that the Justice Department's case against the Sunflower registrar was going to trial in federal court in Greenville. We put on our best clothes and took a couple of carloads of high school kids to watch the trial. The case was well prepared and the federal judge, even though picked by Eastland, was professional to all witnesses, black and white. The Department of Justice lawyer had called as witnesses many whites who had successfully registered to vote, but who were unable to read at all, as they embarrassedly admitted in court. They were asked to read back their own alleged applications but couldn't; they had to admit that the registrar or someone else did the application for them, or sometimes couldn't remember how they got registered. Also called as witnesses were some blacks who were college graduates but who were failed by the registrar; in court they were quite articulate and displayed a far better understanding of the Mississippi constitution than the registrar himself. When put on the stand the registrar fumbled all over the application and completely mucked it up; he was not able to interpret even simple passages in the Mississippi constitution.

The registrar and his high-level lawyer (probably the state attorney general or his assistant) were on the defensive and outmaneuvered at every turn of the trial. It was fun to watch, but we kept a respectful silence, since the lawyer had warned us that this federal judge allowed no breach of decorum in his courtroom. The Department of Justice lawyer was low key but very effective, and the whole day was a great lesson to all of us who attended. We all talked about it at lunch and on the way home. The Freedom Schools taught a lesson about it. The lawyer told us after the trial not to get our hopes up and he said he didn't expect anything from this crony of Eastland's. However, by the time the judge gave his ruling in the late spring the times had changed with the passage of the Voting Rights Act, and the federal judge granted the Justice Department everything it had asked. The registrar was ordered to register every applicant over twenty-one in the county with no delays or further subterfuge. It was a huge defeat for the state of Mississippi, since the ruling went much further than even the Voting Rights Act in its insistence on immediate action by the registrar.

With this court case and several school-desegregation cases in the final stages by early winter, officials in the state in general, and Sunflower County in particular, were in discernible retreat. The FBI was now a little more cool and distant in its dealings with local law enforcement; cases were being prepared against Sheriff Rainey and his criminal gang; the Mississippi congressmen had some one hundred and fifty of their colleagues lined up at some level of involvement to challenge their seating in the House. In the county we were now permanent fixtures in three towns and the level of local black participation was far stronger than anything the whites had expected. Now a daily mood of defiance and even confrontation from the young black people was discernible, something the Sunflower County bosses had never experienced in their lives. The white power structure was cracking and the once-confident county leaders clearly did not have a clue what to do about it. Under these circumstances white frustration grew and it was only a matter of time before the KKK types took out their frustrations on us. Probably because of the benign attitude Parker had towards the Klan, Sunflower was always the hub of KKK activity.

On Christmas Eve Sunflower police "chief" Speedy Miles and two cronies got drunk and parked in front of our house. They then loudly demanded that I come out; they said they had a "Christmas present" for me. Surprised by this purported show of kindness by the hitherto hostile Miles, suspecting that his "gift" might not be very agreeable, and since I had certainly nothing to give or say to him in return, I declined his invitation to come to the car to receive his largess. Miles showed his great disappointment by unleashing a string of unkind remarks about me, not in keeping with the Christmas spirit, I might add, before he drove off, swerving his car all over the narrow street. Lucky for him he was the only cop in town or someone would surely have arrested him for drunken driving. Subsequently that night some young friends of his threw firecrackers at the house, to help us celebrate, I suppose. The following night at one o'clock in the morning a Molotov cocktail was launched at our house and the house was set on fire. Willie D. Smith heard the "pop," and he, Willie Drain and I rushed out and put out the fire with our handy fire extinguishers. The damage was slight that night, but a few nights later Miles and his friends had greater success. The SNCC car was always parked next to the house; late at night towards the end of December they for once used some measure of stealth and quietly set it on fire; the car burned to a crisp before we were alerted and we were unable to use the fire extinguishers to any useful effect. That was a huge loss since now we in Indianola-Sunflower were down to just the one car I had brought from Los Angeles. The many drivers of my car and the conditions in which we had to speed around the county caused it to be in disrepair frequently; fortunately black Indianola had an excellent repairman, Guy McComb, who was very friendly to us and gave us great service at basically his cost. The burned-out hulk of the SNCC car remained in the Sunflower driveway for many months.

In the late fall we attended several COFO and SNCC meetings. There was a very large COFO meeting in Hattiesburg in November and shortly after we went to a week-long SNCC retreat at a Methodist church school campus in Waveland, Mississippi, on the Gulf Coast very close to New Orleans. John, Fred Winn and I went, maybe Charley Scattergood too (I am pretty sure McLaurin skipped that meeting), but we didn't stay the whole week. The sessions focused on the relationship of staff with the local people. There was a division between Bob Moses and Jim Forman at the meeting; Forman seemed to want SNCC to become a more disciplined and centralized body, almost like a traditional cadre party. There was a strong sympathy for Cuba from all sides, but the question as to whether the SNCC organization had to imitate the Cuban party was not settled. It was at this meeting that Guyot made the impassioned speech that I feared would end with an inadvertent blow on my head since I was in the pew directly in front of him. My guess is that he strongly supported Moses's position that SNCC's role was to support the buildup of local organizations. John Harris and I were also strong supporters of that position, although we spoke hardly at all. We had worked in that direction for some months and felt that many local people were already very strong and providing direction to the movement; thus facilitating their role was much more important than building up our internal organization. I myself had observed for a few months prior to the summer the baleful fate of a cadre party like the Communist Party in Los Angeles, who spent far more time in meaningless internal debates than in doing things. SNCC was very far from that state of affairs in November 1964, but the week-long internal debate was not a healthy sign nor was the desire by some to imitate the Cuban party. I said very little, but mostly listened. Some nights John, Fred and I left the retreat meetings to sample New Orleans and its famous Bourbon Street, which was a far more enjoyable form of rest and recuperation.

At that retreat, however, the issue of sexism that permeated SNCC, just like any other contemporary left organization, was first brought up openly. An anonymous paper written by two veteran SNCC women, called the "The Position of Women in SNCC" was circulated and brought up for discussion. The reception by men in SNCC was cool at best and embarrassing at worst. The most egregious remark was made by Stokely Carmichael. We were all seated in a large room with chairs in a circle. He got into the middle of the circle, lay down and then said, "I think the position of women in SNCC should be prone." He got his desired laughs from only a minority of the men, and some of the women were furious. After an impassioned discussion of an hour or so Bob Moses got up and gave a soft-spoken but stirring rebuke to Stokely asking the people to think about how much women in SNCC sacrificed and how much leadership women in Mississippi provided; the congressional challenge was in fact led by three women. He then pointedly compared how much more seriously Cuba took the role of women than certain people in SNCC. Carmichael was now isolated in his position and the discussion took a more positive tone, but the general feeling was that race, not gender, was the key issue.

While excluding whites from SNCC was not brought up at that meeting the feeling was often expressed that whites should not be in leadership roles. I personally agreed with that position, seeing myself as more of a cadre and foot soldier and I was quite happy with the leadership of John and Mac and the increasingly important leadership role many local people like Oscar Giles played in Sunflower and Otis Brown in the young people's movement in the county. The baggage of a hundred years of white supremacy would only be overthrown by local people, not by a second group of carpetbaggers from the North, however well-meaning. I saw myself more after this meeting as a temporary presence in Mississippi and was more committed to fostering local leadership in Sunflower.

At this meeting, or possibly a subsequent one, Moses presciently took the idea of excluding whites from leadership roles one step further. He also added that future leaders of SNCC should be born and raised in Mississippi and not have had a college education. The idea of excluding whites was fine with Carmichael, but since he was from New York and highly educated these last conditions proposed by Moses were infuriating to him; Carmichael had been campaigning to replace John Lewis as chairman of SNCC and he saw his ambitions to become the next head of SNCC stymied, so he lashed out at Bob Moses in a long, rambling, vituperative speech. As was usual in SNCC nothing was settled and in two years' time Carmichael would achieve his ambition to replace Lewis as chairman of SNCC; he then promptly did exclude whites from the organization, prompting a furious Fannie Lou Hamer to resign from SNCC. It then became a very narrow cadre organization with decreasing influence, until its demise before the end of the decade. But I was long gone from Mississippi by then. We did see Carmichael in Los Angeles in late 1966 or early 1967; he came as principal speaker at a rally in support of John Harris, who had been arrested for criminal syndicalism; the crime was passing out leaflets calling to account a killer cop. Stokely had never been a close friend to John, but his solidarity with victims of racist injustice was second to none. So my last memories of Carmichael are very positive; unfortunately he died young at fifty-seven.

On January 4, 1965, I got up at the crack of dawn. It was a cold morning in Sunflower; overnight we had had a dusting of snow. This was the day of the congressional challenge in Washington and in solidarity we in Sunflower County had planned a big demonstration at the courthouse in Indianola. I walked the three blocks from Annie Mae King's House to the church to meet the people of Sunflower who would be shuttled down in my car. There was nobody at the corner when I got there and I thought, "What if we call a demonstration and nobody comes?" After a long fifteen minutes a lady came running toward me; finally someone to join me! Then another lady, and then, as if on signal, came dozens of people. The car was full and I waited for the second run; it only took thirty minutes. The kids finally got out of bed, more ladies from the town; some older guy with a car from the town helped take the loads of people now waiting on that once lonely corner. Probably as many as one hundred people came from Sunflower. I went in the last shuttle and joined the Indianola people who were rallying under John's leadership in the black section. That day students led by Bridges Randall from the Mississippi Valley State, an-all-black college in nearby Leflore County, organized a boycott. A large contingent of college students and some teachers from that school joined us in Indianola. I fell in with their contingent as we marched to the Courthouse. When I got to the courthouse John had organized a

On January 4, 1965 one-third of the House of Representatives mounted an
unprecedented challenge to the fraudulent election of three Mississippi
Congressmen, whose election virtually excluded blacks. Over five hundred people
picketed the Sunflower County Courthouse in support. In this photo the author,
Jim Dann, marches in the demonstration.

picket line five-hundred strong that surrounded the courthouse.
Most of the people were from Indianola and Sunflower but a strong
contingent came from Ruleville and some from a few other places.
Charles McLaurin arrived around noon. Energized by the crowd he
boldly stood on the courthouse steps, which were normally excluded
for blacks, and gave his version of the "I Have a Dream" speech. The

This was the first demonstration ever in front of the County's bastion of authority. People marched in droves from the black section of Indianola. At the head of the march is Otis Brown, defiantly calling for freedom in Swahili, "Uhuru"; Mckinley Mack carries the national flag around a courthouse that had made a point of displaying the battle flag of the Confederate slave-owner rebellion. Charles McLaurin is behind them. McLaurin then bravely mounted the steps of the white-only side to deliver a long speech to the crowd, while the deputy sheriffs looked on. For fear of giving ammunition to the challengers in Washington, no attempt was made to suppress the demonstration.

sun was ever so pale that day in Indianola and the day never did warm up but the energy of the crowd at this the first demonstration at the county courthouse was red hot. The sheriff was watching more discreetly than normal, and he gave us no trouble.

The last thing the embattled Mississippi delegation wanted was any trouble back home to interfere with their seating. There was no chance Hamer, Devine and Gray would be seated, but we wanted the all-white delegation not to be seated and new fair elections called. When the vote was called some one hundred and forty-nine members—about a third of the House—voted to not seat the Mississippi delegation. Although the racist delegation was seated, the House allowed for forty days of depositions and evidence to be brought to a hearing for the formal challenge to be heard. President Johnson did not support the challenge, but considering that the white Mississippians had all supported Goldwater he did not see that they had much of a claim on him, and he did not go out of his way to back them too strongly. He invited Hamer, Gray and Devine and seven other Mississippi Freedom Democratic Party delegates to his inauguration; they all attended. This calculated snub to the white Mississippi power structure was as far as Johnson would go, but to go so far as to not seat congressmen, even if they had been elected undemocratically, would have been a major precedent that neither he nor the House leadership was prepared to take. After all, probably half the House, not only those from the South but also many northern big-city Democrats, did not have very clean hands when it came to honest elections. Johnson's own first elections in the thirties to the House in Texas were carried thanks to his having swept the "graveyard vote." In Indianola we broke up the demonstration in the early afternoon and somehow got the people home. John and I and the other SNCC workers celebrated at the White Rose Café.

The MFDP mobilized one hundred and fifty lawyers mainly from the National Lawyers Guild to come to Mississippi to immediately begin taking depositions. We had already lined up people that fall and when they came to Sunflower County to take the formal

Indianola, January 4, 1965: As the community of Indianola marched through the black section to the Courthouse, police cars, formerly so threatening, were a mere curiosity and had no effect on the participation.

depositions they could choose from about a hundred witnesses to interview and depose. So in January and most of February we were busy lining up and shuttling witnesses for the lawyers to depose. The White Citizens' Council and the KKK were unusually quiet in this period and the cops and deputies left us alone to do our work. No doubt word had come from on high that this was no time to do violence to us or our witnesses. The powers in the state were on the defensive and every effort was made to keep their ignorant base in check at least until the expected hearings. But these hearings were delayed for months by procedural issues and, by March, the KKK's patience was wearing thin and they were itching to be back to business as usual.

The hearings in Congress were delayed by Johnson's allies until September and nothing came out of all that testimony and three thousand pages of depositions. Johnson didn't want this diversion; he had a much more ambitious agenda with Medicare, Head Start

Charles McLaurin speaks to the crowd at the January 4 picket. His speech was upbeat, hopeful, not angry. He took freely from Martin Luther King's famous "I Have a Dream" speech, talking of the bright future when integration will finally come to Sunflower County.

and many other progressive programs, which in scope rivaled those of the New Deal. The white Mississippi members staunchly opposed all these programs but they were now marginalized in their influence, while the more progressive House members saw Johnson's ambitious domestic agenda as more important than unseating the racists. So the challenge sort of just petered out. At the same time the Council of Federated Organizations or COFO was in the process of being unwound. The Mississippi Freedom Democratic Party really had taken over all its functions, the NAACP had formally withdrawn from COFO and anti-communist attacks on lawyers from the National Lawyers Guild had taken their toll on the more timid members; SNCC by contrast only grew all the more militant and less interested in coalitions. The original coalition now had little in common and there seemed to be no more need for COFO; it was gone by July.

In this period we in Sunflower County made our own foray into coalition building. We had heard that there was to be an organizational meeting of Young Democrats in Jackson called by the Hodding Carter element as an effort to build a Democratic Party in Mississippi loyal to President Johnson. Scattergood and I took two carloads of teenagers down to the meeting and we just walked in uninvited. The young white people there were mostly college students or of that age and almost all male; they were a little taken aback by our interracial presence, not to speak of the fact we had more female attendees than they. But the organizers did not object as we took seats near the front and joined the discussion. I suppose many of these young people were of good will and just never had been in a meeting with black people before; others were mindful that the days of a segregated party in Mississippi were over and we had to be tolerated. We in turn were perhaps overly strident and demanded that past sins of racism had to be addressed before any organizational questions could be tackled. The organizers remained polite, but really did not want us there; however, we were too uncompromising to build any kind of coalition. The meeting broke up without anything accomplished. The kids on the way home were happy with our militancy; they had spoken to young whites as equals and didn't give an inch to them in the discussions. Since most of our kids were from Sunflower, our many afternoon discussions of politics had prepared them well to debate white university students. This was unprecedented in both life experiences and ideological outlook between our kids and the university students and well worth the effort. The gulf, a legacy of racism, in any event was too wide for a coalition to be built at that time. By this time I myself after nine months in Mississippi found it impossible to relate to these clean-cut young students with their button-down shirts, mostly from "Ole Miss." Instead when we got back to Sunflower we had a great evening enjoying each other's company and just hanging out at Mrs. King's house.

It was probably one of our last good times there. In the early hours of March 5 the Ku Klux Klan struck the house with a

Two months after the courthouse demonstration the firebombers struck and burned the Freedom School to the ground. The flames destroyed the large collection of books on black history. In this photo a schoolchild finds one that survived the wreckage.

The police and Indianola Fire Department looked on as the blaze finished off the Freedom School. Firemen never even hooked up their hoses, while policemen prevented the people with fire extinguishers from approaching the building when there was possibly still time. No arrests were ever made, except for protesting Civil Rights Workers.

barrage of their military-grade tear gas canisters, breaking many windows and rendering the house uninhabitable for some time. We fled that night to Indianola and, fearing the worst for the Freedom School, we got John at Mrs. Magruder's and rushed over to the school. It was completely engulfed in flames; the flames were easily twenty feet high by the time we got there and so the fire extinguishers we brought from Mrs. Magruder's house would have been useless. In any event the "fire department" was already there with the cops and they wouldn't let us near the school. The firemen sat around joking with the cops while the school burned and only connected their hoses to prevent the spread of the fire. Not only the school was lost but the four-hundred-book library as well.

The next day the cops were still happily guarding the smoldering ruins as Charley Scattergood and I approached. They stopped us, saying it was a crime scene; Charley, then incensed with this hypocrisy, accused them of setting the fire. This they didn't seem inclined to deny, but as a crowd of local people joined in they felt threatened and arrested Charley and me. By this time I was shouting at them too and when they handcuffed me they tightened the handcuffs behind my back to the point where I lost feeling in my hands; then they beat me with their batons. As we got out of the cop car near the jail Scattergood went limp, refusing to move; I tried to get him to walk with me to the jail, but he refused to budge. Chief Alexander then showed his cruel and evil side as he directed the cops, who savagely beat him with batons and kicks; Scattergood was bleeding all over as they dragged him feet first, his head banging on the curbs and up the steps to the jail.

Soon a black doctor from Greenville, summoned by John Harris, came to the jail to treat Scattergood's wounds. Charley was in such bad shape that he wasn't even put in our usual cell, but in some room on the first floor. After the doctor treated Scattergood he came to see me. I still had no feeling in my right hand, but otherwise only had minor bruises. Nevertheless the doctor put a great deal of bandages on my arm and gave me a sling, more to make a political statement than for any medical reasons; he indicated to me privately that the nerve damage was only temporary and my feeling would come back. The sheriff, embarrassed by all the excessive violence of Alexander's cops, released Scattergood that day and I was bailed out the next day with my arm still in the sling. On Church Street upon my release dozens of people came up to me expressing anger and sympathy for my injuries, which by that time didn't bother me at all. But I liked the attention. I didn't remove the bandages and sling until that night.

A few days later after getting my suitcase from Sunflower in order to move back to Indianola I was dropped off by someone in front of Mrs. Magruder's house. At that moment some white guy I didn't know pulled up in his car and yelled at me, "Moving out?" I answered, "No, moving in." At that response he jumped out of his car, fists flying at me, ready to do me as the cops had done to Scattergood a few days earlier. He was a deputy of some kind and had no doubt heard of the beating given to Scattergood; probably he expected me to go limp so he could have some fun. But I was in no mood to take any lumps and slugged him back, giving him back as many punches as he dished at me. Neither of us were great pugilists and there was no chance of a knockout blow by either, but some kids gathered around shouting at him and he got scared and jumped into his car and drove off followed by a hail of stones. He was well known in the neighborhood since his black maid, whom he had been intending to pick up, lived near Mrs. Magruder's house. We filed a complaint with the police and FBI, but they just laughed it off.

Nearby Mrs. Magruder's house was the freedom office, which we had occupied since the early fall, and now we moved our headquarters there; it was fine for staff meetings and some classes but we couldn't hold mass meetings there. None of our troubles in Sunflower County got any national press or attention. By this time the nation was watching the events in Selma, Alabama. For some time now SNCC had been working on a project there, a town as oppressive as any in Mississippi. The Southern Christian Leadership Conference or SCLC was also active in Selma and to some extent both groups worked together. As the oppression led by a brutish sheriff, Jim Clark, worsened in February 1965 the SCLC decided to hold a march from Selma to Montgomery, the state capital, to garner national attention. The SNCC staff in the town feared the worst, but John Lewis typically put his life on the line and agreed to co-lead the march.

On March 7, the day I got released with my minor injuries, John Lewis and others were far more seriously injured during a savage attack by Sheriff Jim Clark, his deputized thugs and vicious state troopers under orders by the arch-racist governor of Alabama, George Wallace, to suppress the march; the marchers had been kneeling in prayer on a blocked bridge that was supposed to be their route for a march to the state capitol in Montgomery for voters' rights. After this atrocity many SNCC workers left Mississippi for Selma to lend a hand, but none of us from Sunflower County went since we were still under the gun with the burning of the Freedom School and nobody could be spared. There were tensions in Selma between SNCC and SCLC, but the utter savagery of the Selma lawmen, egged on by Wallace, forced everyone to work together and captured the sympathy of the nation.

We too in Indianola gathered around Mrs. Magruder's television set every night to watch the network news as thousands of sympathizers from all over the country flooded the town. The racist thugs in Selma murdered a Unitarian minister on March 11 and the protests around the country escalated. As over a thousand black students from Alabama and many more people from elsewhere—my brother David, for instance, came down from Massachusetts for the march—gathered in Selma and in the capital city of Montgomery, President Johnson was forced to act. With characteristic self-confidence and strong leadership Johnson gave a national address, finally putting himself firmly on the side of the demonstrators. National Guard troops were put under federal command, marshals were mobilized, injunctions tied the hands of Wallace and Clark and the promised march from Selma to Montgomery would get protection from federal troops. The second march did take place on March 21, but in the course of it a KKK gang killed a white woman who was shuttling marchers right under the nose of FBI agents who were supposed to have been monitoring that very terrorist cell. Earlier Johnson had made it publicly clear that he had lost all patience with Governor Wallace and he took the opportunity to force Congress to pass a far-reaching Voting Rights Act, which would finally enforce federal standards for elections and end once and for all the all-white, one-party terrorist states in the Deep South. He ended his speech by taking the anthem of the civil rights movement as his own. We watched amazed as he said "We shall overcome." It was March 14, 1965, and we were in Mrs. Magruder's living room, missing our Freedom School but ready to move on to new paths of struggle.

9

New Hopes
and New Paths of Struggle

··

Now 'tis the spring and weeds are shallow-rooted;
Suffer them now, and they'll o'ergrow the garden,
And choke the herbs for want of husbandry.

HENRY VI Part II

When the breakthrough in voters' rights that we had all worked for came that spring it was immediately sparked by the struggle in Selma, Alabama, but also inspired by our efforts in Mississippi as well as four years of struggle in other parts of the Deep South. It was not clear to us at the time that the Voting Rights Act would change things on the ground any more than the Civil Rights Act of 1964 had. Some of us felt a need to look for new paths of struggle since we didn't have the patience of Mrs. Hamer to keep on keeping on. The war against Vietnam was one opportunity since the United States going to war for "freedom" was such obvious hypocrisy given the totalitarian state of Mississippi that all of SNCC was quick to draw the connection and saw the need to oppose that war. Those of us in Sunflower County also wanted to weigh in concretely on behalf of the peace movement. In March we in Indianola decided to charter a bus to Washington, DC, so that the high school kids we had been working with could go and join the April 18 March on Washington to protest the Vietnam War. It was to be the first major national protest of the war and was sponsored by SNCC and the Students for a Democratic Society (SDS).

A low-level conflict had started in South Vietnam in 1956-58 after the CIA-backed dictatorship of Ngo Dinh Diem canceled the reunification elections with North Vietnam. The corrupt and brutal rule of Diem and his family alienated every sector of society and the National Liberation Front had emerged to fight him. Increasing numbers of United States Special Forces troops and CIA agents were unable to keep Diem's forces from losing ground in the period 1958-1963. On November 2, 1963, the United States opted for direct rule of South Vietnam through Ambassador Henry Cabot Lodge; the CIA organized a coup, executed Diem and his brother and installed a series of generals to be the front men for the US embassy. This meant that now many more US troops, including draftees in the regular army, had to be sent to Vietnam to prop up the puppet state. By the time Kennedy was assassinated later that month there were already about twenty thousand troops from the United States in Vietnam. In a year Johnson was to multiply that number by ten and extend the air war to North Vietnam, but still with no success on the ground in the South, since now seasoned North Vietnamese regulars boosted the forces of the National Liberation Front to match the United States troop buildup.

As the US casualties mounted and the cruel bombing of civilians shocked the world protests began. Students for a Democratic Society took the lead in the United States and called for a National March on Washington for April 18, 1965. SNCC was listed as a sponsor of the march and Bob Moses was to be the principal speaker at the rally. Herschel went to some effort to get funding and to charter a bus just for the Indianola people and it was filled with high school kids from Indianola and Sunflower. Fred and Scattergood and maybe some others went with the kids in the bus.

John, Karen and I drove in my car to Washington, since we thought to stay for a few days after the march with some friends of John.

The numbers in Washington exceeded anyone's expectations. Some twenty-five thousand filled the mall in front of the Washington Monument. The rally was held on the steps to the Washington Monument across the mall from the Capitol. Phil Ochs, the leftist folk singer, sang freedom and anti-war songs but many in the crowd demanded that he sing his sarcastic song "Love Me I'm a Liberal"; he was reluctant because this would embarrass Senator Gruening from Alaska who was to be the liberal anti-war speaker at the rally. Ochs finally sang the song much to the joy of the crowd and later the senator defended himself and liberalism to tepid applause. The final speaker was Bob Moses, who, to standing ovations, gave the most serious indictment of liberal hypocrisy when he said that Mississippi was really just a mirror in which you could more clearly see what all American society was like. The rally was a great experience for us all, especially for the kids from Indianola, who had never been outside of the Delta; now they were in the midst of a crowd of so many protestors, this time mostly white and most welcoming to them.

They went back on the bus that evening. We stayed with some of John Harris's friends from his days at Howard and we talked with them that night and for the next day or two. The only one I remember was Tom Kahn, who was quite cynical about SDS and the anti-war movement. He was like Lowenstein, a Cold War liberal who was now on the outs with the new more radical SDS leadership, and he told us he had no use for them or even for SNCC.

When we returned to Indianola a momentous event had happened in our absence. The federal court order had come through and now the registrar had to register every applicant. The Voting Rights Act would not be law until August 6, so Sunflower County was to be a precursor of what was to happen throughout the Deep South—everyone could now vote and the registrar could only record their registration and no longer be a judge of the applicant's "worthiness." Hundreds of black residents were now at the courthouse and applying and Jim Forman was there to temporarily direct the project; he brought with him more than half a dozen new volunteers from the North to beef up our forces. Forman was none too happy with John's and my extended absence, and for the next few days we all worked double time trying to get the people to the courthouse. Possibly up to a thousand black people were all of a sudden allowed to register. There was a lot of confusion and the small freedom office was packed with so many newcomers and so many people trying to get the registration moving as quickly as possible. In the course of those hectic days the feelings of some of those who had been there a year were hurt and toes got stepped on. Forman left after a day or two and John had to try to solve some internal disputes while at the same time registering so many new voters; the resultant tension took its toll on the project.

During this time of confusion there were inevitably some internal disagreements as to how to proceed in this unprecedented situation and to John and me it seemed better if the project thinned out a bit. John and I told everyone that we would be leaving the Indianola project to work with the Head Start program in Jackson; Charles Scattergood also said he was leaving at that time. Probably the burning of the Freedom School and the attack on the house in Sunflower had a bigger effect on the three of us than we could admit, even to ourselves, and we needed to get away and do something different. It was not, however, the best time to make that announcement to the people on the project; there were some who even called us sellouts, but there were others like Otis Brown who were supportive of us and ready to take leadership of the project. As usual Charles McLaurin was also personally very supportive of John and me and said he thought this new Head Start program offered another good venue for struggle and encouraged us in this new path. McLaurin was still in school, but in the summer he again took the active leadership in Sunflower County.

Annie Mae King returned at that time and had her house cleaned, re-windowed and once again made habitable. She told me that I could stay there with her any time I wanted to, but it would no longer be a place for the kids to hang out. I had heard of some complaints from the community during the spring to the effect that I was not active enough in chaperoning the kids and the teen-aged boys and girls were taking advantage of her house. There was some truth to that and indeed I had been reluctant to oversee the kids, whom I had treated more as friends and colleagues than as kids, but they were in fact youngsters, between fifteen and eighteen years old, and the adults in the community may have felt that I was not responsible enough. People were very mild with me and just gave out hints, but my guess is that Mrs. King got an earful when she returned and that is why she said I was welcome to stay with her as much as I wanted to but her house was not to be a kids' hang-out any more. I understood and accepted that. Although I would now be staying near Jackson mostly, I did come up to Sunflower County many times in the next four months and stayed with her. She was as kind and hospitable as ever, and now I had the additional benefit of her excellent cooking.

In May after John and I were gone from Indianola the KKK burned Mrs. Magruder's house to the ground and that same night another set of targets was attacked as well, including Oscar Giles's grocery store.[1] Luckily the store was only moderately damaged, and he was shortly back in business. Mrs. Magruder had been extremely courageous in having us stay as her guests, cooking for

---

1. In 2000 Sheriff Hollowell told Fred Winn and me a highly improbable story that the attacks that night had all been the work of a single black man upset that his girlfriend was involved in the civil rights movement. According to him the arsonist then escaped to Chicago. It is possible that Hollowell believed this story that was maybe fed to him by others, but I certainly didn't. That motive for those targets is not only incredible and illogical, but also the simultaneity of the attacks rules out any single arsonist. Indeed the mode of operation, the choice of weapons (firebombs) and the choice of targets were exactly what we had seen before with the KKK attacks all during the past year. The only logical conclusion is that the KKK thugs, likely with the help of cops and deputies, were again responsible.

Mrs. Irene Magruder's house front view, May 1, 1965, after it was firebombed. Irene Carter Magruder was the first person in Indianola to house civil rights workers.

us and cleaning up after us. Often people from out of town would just show up for a night or two and her hospitality was always warm and complete. It was a comfortable house, warm and cozy; she had a television, which everybody on the project watched, and a phone, which was rare in the black community and thus very important to us. The loss of Mrs. Magruder's house put additional stress on the remaining Indianola project since now most people had to sleep in the small freedom office; consequently a number of the newer volunteers left during the course of that summer, but Otis Brown and some other of his friends now took over the functions of the northern volunteers and the Indianola and Sunflower movements suffered little. They made slow but steady progress in the years ahead in voting, desegregation and eventually elections. Otis was to run unsuccessfully in 1967 for mayor of Sunflower.

By the time of this last KKK outrage John and I were completely immersed in helping organize the first Head Start program in the state and its first integrated federal program. We were initially headquartered in a small campus in the town of Edwards just out-side of Jackson. The name of the organization we worked with was the Child Development Group of Mississippi. It was headed by a dynamic psychoanalyst from New York named Tom Levin. He was short fit man of forty-one, always smiling, very well spoken and a good, sympathetic listener. To help run the program he brought in about half a dozen young white women from New York, and he recruited about the same number of young black women from Talledega College, a black college in Alabama. When we got to Edwards this core group of Levin and a dozen young college-age women were already setting up shop and organizing the financial end, but they didn't know a great deal about the reality of rural Mississippi.

Tom Levin had come to Mississippi the same summer as I did to serve as part of the Doctors for Human Rights that operated out of Jackson along with the National Lawyers Guild. When he returned to New York at the end of the summer he wanted to do more for Mississippi and saw an opportunity with the new War on Poverty that Johnson was then pushing through Congress. One of the anti-poverty programs initiated in 1965 was the Head Start program that would prepare poor kids for school, by taking pre-schoolers and starting them off in a school setting. The programs were to be run by a local board, which could be independent of state and local government. The Office of Economic Opportunity in Washington would provide funds and national oversight, but local control was to be emphasized. Levin applied to that office for a grant and then through Jim Forman approached SNCC to have the Council of Federated Organizations or the Mississippi Freedom Democratic Party run the local boards. At an SNCC staff meeting in the winter Levin asked for SNCC's help, but suspicion and resentment of Johnson ran deep and Levin could get no official endorsement. However, John and I and one or two others spoke to Levin privately and the two of us expressed interest in working with him in Indianola. We were always looking for new ways to promote the struggle. He took our names, but we didn't hear from him for a while. Meanwhile he got his staff together and through them approached some COFO and MFDP local projects. With these projects and through word of mouth a plan for eighty-four centers in twenty-four counties was presented to Washington and the Office for Economic Opportunity was asked to fund a pilot project for Mississippi for the summer. They came through with $1.5 million, Levin got sponsorship from a local black college to avoid any state control and then he contacted John and me to join him. The project was to be headquartered at an abandoned black junior college in the town of Edwards, about twenty miles from Jackson.

The choice of Head Start sites had been haphazard; it depended on who had contacted whom and how. As a result a number of movement counties with strong SNCC presence were left out. On the other hand some counties were included that never had a significant SNCC presence; in those places some local leaders had asked someone else that they be part of Head Start. It turned out that Sunflower County was left out; we don't know why, whether through oversight or because someone in SNCC, not John or I, had been contacted and said no to the person from the Child Development Group of Mississippi. In any event Sunflower was not in the original proposal of twenty-four counties given to the Office of Economic Opportunity and now could not be included. When we met with Levin in late April he asked John and me to be district directors; there were to be five district directors responsible for coordination between central staff in Edwards and the local school sites. I got central Mississippi; John got the south of the state on the Gulf of Mexico Coast, including the big cities of Biloxi and Gulfport. I asked Levin if something could now be done to get Sunflower County in. The best he could do was to allow me to set up a Head Start school in the town of Leland, just outside of the Sunflower County line in Washington County, located fifteen miles from Indianola. Washington County was to be part of my district.

Indianola people could then staff the Leland Center and Indianola preschoolers would be bused in from Indianola, although I had to organize all this and find a site.

My central district ran from Leland in the north over one hundred miles to Vicksburg in the south along the Mississippi River and then east to Jackson and Canton in the center of the state. I was responsible for about ten sites from the most urban, Jackson, to the most rural in Issaquena County, which had no town of any size, just tiny rural hamlets in the woods. Some centers like the one in Canton had experienced COFO veterans on the board; Rev. James McRee led the board and he was a strong, confident leader who easily took command of the schools there and had everything running smoothly. Other counties like Sharkey and Issaquena had not had a significant SNCC presence and there were no civil rights veterans to help, which meant I had to do all the leg work. The local black leaders in Sharkey and Issaquena counties had contacted the Child Development Group on their own, I believe, through McRee and asked to be included. As a federal program Head Start had to be integrated, so an effort was made to get poor white children in the program. But we had no good way to contact the whites except through the papers and none ever attended in my district, nor as far as we can remember in any district. In general the white power structure was totally hostile to the program and any white parent having their child attending would have been totally ostracized. The whole setup in any event was very rushed; it was a question of weeks between when the grant was approved until classes opened and many who could have been included were not.

For those in the program there were very significant benefits. The hundreds of black preschoolers who attended in my district got two hot meals a day, as well as all their instructional materials from pencils and scissors to blackboards and paint. They were all seated at brand new comfortable desks in large roomy and well-lit rooms. They were taught by teachers who cared about them and treated them well. The basic curriculum was numbers, alphabet and a lot of art and paper construction; if possible they were taught to write their own names. The curriculum was far more creative, individualized and more advanced than they would see at the segregated schools, and the classrooms were more comfortable and better equipped than most public schools are today in California.

The teachers were only required to have graduated from high school and few had any further education; the aides who helped them had no educational requirements. Almost all teachers and aides in my district were women. They were paid one hundred dollars a week for teachers and ninety dollars a week for aides. The one hundred dollars a week was the maximum salary paid anyone in the Child Development Group program; that was the pay rate for Levin, the central staff and for us district directors. Since the going rate outside of the program for black women was three dollars a day with a full week rare, for most women in the Child Development Group program the salary was about ten times what they could have made working for local whites. In addition there were none of the usual insults from the bosses that blacks had to put up with; people in the Child Development program were treated with respect. This was a liberating experience for the women involved and the money was, of course, a great help in the household. No doubt voter registration, desegregation and Freedom Schools had a long-range revolutionary aspect, but of all the things I was involved with, Head Start provided the most immediately palpable results in bettering the condition of the people then and there.

The promised eighty-four centers didn't all materialize. Probably half to two thirds of that number actually came together; in my district the ten centers were less than in the original proposal to the Office of Economic Opportunity, but they all ended up working. We district directors had to handle coordination between the sites and the central office in Jackson. In theory the local boards picked the sites, rented the space and hired teachers and aides. This was the case in Madison County where Rev. James McRee took charge and had everything functioning well; also in Jackson and

Vicksburg the local boards and leadership did these things. All I had to do for these centers was see that the desks and instructional materials were delivered, carry the paychecks to the centers and look after security. We also got all the teachers to Edwards for a three- or four-day period of initial training. In Sharkey, Issaquena and Leland the leadership was either weaker or new and besides what I did for the other counties I had to rent the space and guide the process of hiring. It seems there was no problem getting students in any center and we operated at capacity with little absenteeism and virtually no dropouts. The white school boards universally would not rent space to us, even in the segregated black schools. So we got churches, black-owned community centers and occasionally just a vacant farmhouse to house the centers, but they were all clean, well lit and roomy.

Like the teachers we district directors were paid one hundred dollars a week, but we got the use of brand new air-conditioned cars to go from site to site. And indeed I was on the go almost seven days a week from early morning usually till after dark. I slept mostly at the headquarters in Edwards. There was plenty of dorm space and I had a dorm room to myself. I could eat with the staff if I was around for dinner. If I found myself in the north end of the district late at night I went to Annie Mae King's house in Sunflower, where she always cooked me a nice meal. Sometimes I ate lunch with the kids at the centers; local black women who were aides cooked the meals and bought the food with money provided by the Child Development Group program and the meals were very nutritious and delicious. I had little to spend my one hundred dollars a week on and mostly saved it for college.

During my little off-time in Edwards I made some close friendships with the staffers there; one I remember was Duff Campbell, a beginning law student from New York who was Levin's top assistant. She was helpful to me in many ways and was good company in Edwards. I also made some friends among the college students from Talledega, who worked very hard at the center and often had a lot of interesting insights. When I was staying at the northern end of the district I saw a lot of Cora Fleming and Thelma Mack; Cora was the head teacher in Leland and was completely dedicated to the Head Start program. I admired the way she organized and ran the center with dedicated leadership and complete integrity. She was thirty-two; a very intelligent lady, she was looking for something different than being a housewife in Indianola. She had not much more than a high school education in the segregated schools, but she quickly took charge of the center and showed great leadership skills as well as being a superb and compassionate teacher to the kids. I met her through her close friend Thelma Mack, whose family had been deeply involved with us in the Indianola struggles that year. Thelma was a teacher at Leland too and very close to Cora, but Thelma recognized that Cora was necessary for the leadership of the center.

Thelma and Cora were examples of the liberating experience the Child Development Group provided black women of the Delta. Both were highly intelligent women and wanted something better than being stuck in Indianola with no better prospects than either an unequal marriage or a job as a maid in some white woman's house. They instead became leaders of the Sunflower County Head Start program with a decent salary and interesting and challenging work. In contrast to the desegregation movement of the last year, young women in their thirties and twenties, both in the central headquarters and in the sites, provided almost all the leadership and direction to the program.

Twice during the summer I visited John Harris in Gulfport for a weekend. It was an interesting experience to see what he was doing since his area was quite different in nature than mine. John's program ran much bigger centers in the coastal cities of Gulfport, Biloxi, Moss Point and Pascagoula.

With many good friends and these nice living arrangements, not to speak of the fine air-conditioned car, it was easy to begin to forget that we were still operating in extremely hostile territory.

Sharkey, Issaquena and Madison counties were KKK-run counties where law enforcement and the white plantation owners were members or supporters of that terrorist group. The Head Start took them and the state White Citizens' Council leaders by surprise in the spring, but they both swung into action against us by the time the program was running. Anguilla in Sharkey County was the scene of a cross-burning near our center on June 25. We had an evening meeting at the center a few days later to discuss the situation. It was a fine summer night and I went out on the porch to get some air and talk privately to one of the teachers. A porch light was on and I stupidly stood next to it. The center was in a vacant farmhouse and there was a large cotton field between it and the road. A couple of shots rang out from across the field, hitting the light and shattering the front windows. We quickly took shelter inside and nothing more came of it. We had, of course, no firearms since it was policy not to have any in the centers or in the cars of staff members. We were defenseless had the KKK chosen to do more that night, but they didn't. I never knew if the gunman was a lousy shot and missed me or a good shot and was just trying to scare me. But in any event I remembered and reviewed the rules McLaurin had taught us about security a year before in Ruleville. No more lights on porches and unshaded windows, and we took care that all the teachers were safely escorted home in those KKK counties.

After that attempt, I was also determined to make sure nobody ever passed me on the highway, as McLaurin also had taught me. This got me into trouble a few days later when I saw a car in the distance trying to catch up with me on Highway 61 in Sharkey County. I sped up and led the car on a high-speed chase almost to Jackson, when the highway patrolman caught up with me and forced me to stop. He knew who I was and was all the more hostile to me as he grabbed me and handcuffed me. He seemed especially upset that I had an air-conditioned car and that he didn't, a fact that he mentioned more than once in between his insults about the Head Start program and civil rights in general. He led me to the

Warren County justice of the peace, who fined me as much as he could, but I had the cash on hand and got back to my car safely and went straight to Edwards to report to Levin. Mississippi had an inordinately high tolerance for speeding and the fines by statue were relatively low and as long as we had twenty-five or fifty dollars in our pockets we could get out. (Earlier in the year John, Scattergood and I led a sheriff's deputy on a one-hundred-mile-an-hour chase for maybe forty miles before a roadblock on the main highway to Jackson was set up just for us and nailed us. We were taken to the Humphreys County courthouse but could pay our way out of that one too.) Nobody wanted to be passed on the highway and shot, nor did we want to be held in jail and released at night as happened to Chaney. So carrying enough cash to pay speeding tickets was a wise precaution.

I told Tom Levin all this and opined that I was especially targeted because of my connection with the Child Development Group. He was sympathetic but, surprisingly to me, reluctant to pay me back for the fine. He eventually did find the money for me; probably it came out of his own pocket, although I didn't know that at the time. He explained that the federal auditors were breathing down his neck and he had to be very careful; paying speeding tickets would not look good to the auditors. Indeed the biggest threat to the Child Development Group of Mississippi that summer was not the KKK but Senator Stennis, who in his capacity as head of the Senate's Appropriations Committee was furious that federal money had got past his watchful eyes to a semi–civil rights group. He was determined to kill the Child Development Group program, as he stated from the Senate floor. In the House in addition two of the congressmen, whose challenges to their flawed election had not even yet been settled, shamelessly went on the warpath against the program, echoing the governor's assertion that it was causing "dissension between the races [sic]." At this point since the money had been already appropriated and President Johnson wouldn't budge on his vision for an integrated Head Start program as the keystone to his War on Poverty, Stennis and his fellow racist Mississippi congressmen were trying to get us on misuse of federal funds.

Not long after that Levin told me that staffers from Stennis's office wanted to see some of our centers for themselves and asked me to be the one to show them around. Naturally I thought Sharkey County would be a good place to meet them so they could see what we had accomplished given the utterly hostile conditions in a place like that. The two portly fellows in dark suits and ties were outwardly friendly when I met them that morning, but did not hide their skepticism about the program. I politely showed them the centers in Anguilla and Rolling Fork. Indeed they could see the desks, the instructional materials, the hot lunches and a full complement of students learning their ABC's. Everyone was working hard and anyone could see at a glance that the money for the centers was being well spent. They saw a vacant farmhouse transformed into a sunny, well-equipped classroom, decorated with student work. They actually seemed satisfied that there was not the expected misuse of funds and that we did much with the little money we got; however, when I detailed the threats and shootings they were not very interested. They were only looking for misuse of federal funds and there was none at all in my centers; indeed few, if any, federal programs were as obviously frugal, doing so much with so little, as ours. I also took them to Madison County, where similarly everything was run frugally and correctly and small churches and community centers were likewise transformed into exemplary classrooms. But at our headquarters in Edwards some stool pigeon had told them that the bookkeeping in the central office was a mess and in violation of federal standards, and Stennis's staffers made much of that. After I left them at headquarters in the afternoon they spent a day more in Edwards poring over the accounts. But of real fraud and corruption they found nothing at all, just sloppy bookkeeping, poorly coordinated financial disbursements and an office staffed with people unfamiliar with the arcane federal guidelines. Levin and his staff may not have been good bookkeepers but their integrity was unquestionable.

Indeed the central office way of handling money had been a mess and that problem had earlier led to some heated messages from Rev. McRee to Levin through me as the willing messenger. The problem was that the first two paychecks to the teachers were incompetently done and many people were not paid for a time. McRee was furious since it seemed that the worst problem was in Madison County. However, I uncovered several serious problems in Sharkey County as well and the central headquarters forgot altogether about paying the teachers and aides in the new centers of Issaquena and Leland/Indianola. I was very critical of this to Levin and eventually that problem got straightened out. I told him that getting the paychecks out correctly had to be first priority in Edwards; after the first few weeks there were no further problems that I was aware of. McRee was less satisfied with the way the central office functioned and wanted changes in the statewide board. In the course of the summer Levin pushed some people off the board to make way for McRee to become the chairman; Levin also took my suggestion that the man in charge of the Issaquena site, whom I enormously respected, be added to the board. (Unfortunately his name is lost to my memory and I could not find any record of him.) Both of these men seemed to like me a lot and asked my opinion on a lot of things that came before the board; they were disenchanted with Levin and increasingly during the course of the summer made that clear to me. They wanted me to take on a bigger role in the central office, but I was reluctant to get involved except to talk to Duff Campbell about specific problems.

My sites in Jackson and Edwards presented little work for me since the schools were on the headquarters campus and central office people took care of most of my duties. Vicksburg likewise was no work for me since it was close, just twenty miles from Edwards. The city of about twenty-five thousand, sixty-five percent black, was located on a bluff overlooking the Mississippi River, and its capture in 1863 was one of Ulysses S. Grant's greatest victories, since that outcome had split the slave-owners' confederacy in two. A century later the SNCC/MFDP workers in Vicksburg had welcomed the Head Start and led the local board; they chose the teachers from among young women activists in that town. From what I could see they were as good teachers as they were committed to the movement. Despite a long history of KKK violence in Vicksburg, including a nineteenth-century massacre of three hundred black residents,[2] there was no violence against our project; the movement activists who ran the program conducted it smoothly, and I had to check in with them no more than a once a week.

In Madison County, where we had, I believe, three centers, I depended entirely on Rev. James McRee. I checked in with him often and if it was suppertime he always asked me to dine with him at his house; perhaps that increased my desire to check in with him. He had a very nice family, maybe four or five kids, and all members of the family were most gracious and hospitable to me no matter what time I arrived. The food was always good and the discussions were always interesting with him. A short, fit, handsome man of about thirty-five or forty, McRee was very intelligent, well read and very earnest about the project; I grew to respect him more and more as the summer progressed. I made sure his centers got first priority on equipment and money to the extent I could influence those matters. While the white power structure in the county tended to be KKK, the blacks were well organized and looked out for the safety of the centers and teachers by means of some form of a self-defense force, the details of which I took care not to inquire into too deeply. I don't remember any serious problems there. The education was first-rate in the centers and once we got the paychecks coming on time the staff worked together under McRee like a well-oiled machine.

In Leland Cora Fleming and Thelma Mack picked the teachers and aides from among Indianola women who had supported the

---

2. 1874 Vicksburg massacre

freedom struggle in that town. Thelma and Cora were in their early thirties and picked women from their age group or in their twenties. This provided a higher level of maturity in the staff than had been the case in the desegregation movement and even in most of the other centers. I knew most of the teachers and aides, but not all since our closest Indianola workers in the desegregation campaigns of the past year had tended to be younger and mostly men. The SNCC project in Indianola was less active that summer than it had been when John had led it. It seemed the center of gravity of the movement that summer in Sunflower County had shifted to Sunflower, where Otis Brown led the struggle, and to Ruleville now that Charles McLaurin was in charge again. Therefore many of the movement women in Indianola shifted their focus to the Head Start program. Cora ran a tight ship at the center and everyone respected her; the schools were well attended and the kids got a great education in learning the alphabet and their numbers. I came often to the center, at least every other day, even though it was a one-hundred-thirty mile drive from Edwards.

The two centers in Sharkey County were my most difficult. The local board that had requested the program in that county had melted away after the KKK threats and violence, and only a few teachers and I were willing to take the lead and were there to keep the operations running. The centers were halfway from Edwards to Leland so I could stop by there on the way to Indianola or stay there till the evening as the situation warranted. I was there just about every weekday and sometimes on weekends too. But the courage of the teachers and aides in those two places kept me upbeat and we were able to make sure a quality program, with hot meals and good learning was in place all summer. At my request, the headquarters in Edwards sent from their central staff an experienced young teacher from New York, Ms. Goldberg, to stay in Rolling Fork and help the staff there. She stayed with a local family in town and had to be very careful, as did all the teachers after the violence. The local teachers in those centers were mostly very young and just out of high school—or even still in high school—and Goldberg's experience helped. There was a little dissension among some of the local women and Goldberg's advice helped me to smooth over the differences. In the end those centers were a success.

Issaquena County was probably the most rural in the state. It was wedged against the Mississippi River and had no town even of the size of Sunflower, just tiny hamlets nestled in clearings in the woods. There was not even much in the way of plantations; most of the people were small farmers and ninety percent of them were black. The Child Development Group center was located in the tiny settlement of Glen Allen, just a collection of a dozen houses and a church in the extreme north of the county. To get there from Rolling Fork, itself a town no bigger than Ruleville, you left the paved highway and had to take a twenty-mile dirt road through the woods and past small farms. The deacon of the church was the leader of the project; he was a tall, charismatic, well-built man in his late thirties and owned a small farm in the area. He gave us the church to be the center. Somehow about forty kids were enrolled, transported to the school and regularly attended; they must have been children of the other black farmers in that part of the county, who drove them to the church every morning. The deacon (whose name I cannot recall) hired teachers—who seemed to be girls of high school age—and some local women to be aides, and hot meals were served out of the church. The church was located in a field with no houses around it. His house was maybe half a mile away. The deacon had a sixteen-year-old daughter who was to be one of the teachers, maybe the lead teacher, I am not sure. (In this center I did not inquire if any teacher was a high school graduate; I doubt that there were any women who finished high school and then stayed in that part of the county.) The deacon's family was very hospitable to me and I had supper with them several times; if I stayed late I would sleep at his house to avoid making the trip down that dirt road after dark.

In Issaquena County the ten-percent-minority whites monopolized what government there was; I never saw any sign of local or county law enforcement or officialdom of any kind. It is not likely that that county could support more than a very few poorly paid officials, and the county stretched for seventy-five miles along the river, consisting of just backwoods and small farms connected by nothing but dirt roads. The KKK was probably the real government. The dirt-poor whites, who themselves were small farmers barely getting by, clung to their delusions of white superiority and lived in fear of their black neighbors taking over. The poverty of the blacks in the county was the worst I had ever seen. When I took the volunteer doctors to the center so they could give the kids vaccinations—the Child Development program organized volunteer doctors from the North to come down and vaccinate all the students in the program—they took me aside and said that almost all of the little kids had scabs on their legs from malnutrition.

Yet the school got the same classroom equipment as anywhere else—brand new desks, blackboards, paper pencils and crayons—and there was money for the two hot meals. The women at the school were likely among the best-paid people in the county, black or white.

I never saw any white people driving down that dirt road, but they must have watched me driving in and out in a shiny new air-conditioned car. It was therefore not surprising that envy and jealousy of their black neighbors grew and KKK activists, who maybe hailed from nearby counties, turned it into blind hatred of the center. Although we were careful and observed all the security precautions for the teachers and staff there was no way to protect the church, isolated as it was. I did not want to get into the situation in which I had been involved trying to protect the Sunflower church the previous fall; that had been too close a call and I did not suggest any armed guards. Moreover, if word had ever gotten to the enemies of the Child Development Group that there were firearms in a center, that might have killed the entire program statewide; I did not want to be responsible for that. (If in another county local people defended their centers, as long as I as a staffer was neither involved nor informed about it, this was another matter.) In Glen Allen the church was just locked up at night and everyone hoped for the best.

Early one morning in late summer I got a call in Edwards from someone in Rolling Fork that the church had been burned down. I drove out there immediately and found the deacon inspecting the ruins. There was nothing left, just smoldering ruins. I expected that this was to be the end of that project, but the deacon wanted to continue. He already had plans for constructing a tent on the church grounds. Could I supply them with desks and other school equipment since everything inside the church was also lost? I said I would try. Levin as always was sympathetic. A number of projects elsewhere in the state had folded or never got off the ground so there were plenty of surplus supplies and equipment in Edwards and I arranged to have it trucked up to Glen Allen. After less than a week of conducting classes on the grass we had desks under the tents. The meals were cooked in neighboring houses and the center really never lost a beat. If Stennis's staff had bothered to make the trek down that dirt road they would have found many things wrong, but not the quality of the education or the frugality in the use of government money.

In that summer there were major demonstrations in Jackson. These were started by the Mississippi Freedom Democratic Party to support the congressional challenge but, after the peaceful marchers were cruelly arrested and incarcerated in a stockade, many more came from all over the state, including Annie Mae King from Sunflower. Levin did not want us in the staff to be involved but as the protests grew he looked the other way as we used the Child Development Group cars to shuttle demonstrators to Jackson from one of the staging areas in Edwards. I drove quite a few people there on a daily basis for about a week. One day I drove Jim Forman to the demonstrations. He had been one of the few SNCC leaders supportive of the Child Development program and on the ride he asked me how it was going and seemed satisfied with my take on it. Inevitably some of our staffers also got arrested (about a thousand people in total were arrested and put in the stockade before an injunction stopped the state from arresting any more of the marchers) and Levin put up bail money for the members of his staff. But subsequently the federal auditors went ballistic when they saw the entry "bail fund" on the books; the skids were soon being greased for Levin's dumping.

With McRee and the deacon in Glen Allen I had a reputation of someone who could get things done, especially after the church burning, and they contrasted this with the dysfunction, as they saw it, of the central office. They let me know there was a move afoot to replace Levin and they wanted me to help. I liked Levin, though recognized he was not a good administrator, and tried to avoid that fight. Levin had had the vision and the energy to get the Child Development program off the ground; his mistakes were essentially just administrative and his integrity and good will were never in question. He deserved a softer landing than he got. So as much as I respected McRee and the other board members pushing to dump Levin, I remained non-committal. I had already written to UCLA and told them that I was enrolling for the fall semester. McRee tried to get me to change my mind. But I was ready to leave and didn't want to get involved in something that might hurt Levin; he had always been supportive of me.

The federal auditors and the Office of Economic Opportunity badly wanted Levin replaced, hoping that it would placate Senator Stennis, and the college sponsorship of the Child Development Group of Mississippi was also changing. Leaving with Levin in August were all the college girls from New York and Talledega; there was to be an entirely new team. Headquarters was to be moved from the comfortable college campus in Edwards into an office building in Jackson. John and I stayed on for a few more weeks; it was flattering to me that the new leadership of the Child

Development Group wanted just the two of us to stay during this mass exodus, but staying on permanently would have been challenging with new people to work with, a new setting and an expanded program, with no guarantee of funding. I had always liked working with Rev. McRee, but my course was set, so I prepared my goodbyes. John Harris was also planning to leave so we decided together that we would both go to Los Angeles. After the Watts Rebellion of that summer Los Angeles seemed to be the place to be for the upcoming imagined revolution. So after a week-long stay in New York John and I got one of those drive-aways, a clunker of an Oldsmobile, to drive to LA. It was September 1965 and it would be thirty-five years before I returned to Mississippi, where I had spent the fifteen eventful months described above.

The Child Development Group of Mississippi was to go through many difficult trials and travails in the next few years before the Washington and Mississippi politicians finally killed the program in 1967-68, but I did not know that would happen and left the state feeling good about our accomplishments. For me the four months were an extremely important growing experience. In the first place, for the first time in my life I had administered something, which meant negotiating between individuals and also organizing mundane things that made a program work. Secondly, for the first time I was involved with education and got to see firsthand the rewarding experience that teachers have in their interaction with children, and although it would be another twenty years before I became a teacher myself the experience did affect me. Thirdly and possibly most importantly, for the first time in my life I found myself in a situation working with mostly women, strong and independent women, as colleagues, and this work situation helped me to overcome some of the baggage of the sexist society in which I grew up.

10

Return to Mississippi

··

So we'll live,
And pray, and sing, and tell old tales and laugh...

King LEAR

John and I roomed together in Los Angeles, first briefly with Ridenour in Santa Monica, and then we got a flat together near the beach in Venice. In the fall we attended the Oakland Army Base protests where we met some of our old friends from Mississippi. I wrote to Cora for a time and to the deacon in Issaquena, but otherwise I was not good at keeping up correspondence. When John was arrested for criminal syndicalism in 1966 I called Fannie Lou Hamer for a statement of support, which she graciously gave. But that was the extent of my Mississippi contacts.

In San Francisco, where we often traveled in the sixties, we found a colony of Mississippi veterans with whom we sometimes socialized. There were Fred Winn, Karen Koonan, Janell Glass, Bridges Randle and Willie D. Smith. To one degree or another they were all active in various struggles in the Bay Area during that turbulent decade. Bridges was a leader of the big San Francisco State Strike in 1968. John and I ended up in San Francisco in the early seventies. He went back to Birmingham around 1975; I stayed in San Francisco and finally settled down and made my home there. John and I continued to correspond regularly, talk on the phone and occasionally see each other in the course of the next twenty-five years. There was nobody whose judgment I trusted more than his. In San Francisco in the next decade I also occasionally saw Fred, who now had a plumbing business; Karen, a legal secretary who eventually became head of the National Lawyers Guild; and Janell, a manager for a social service agency. We veterans talked a bit about what was going on in Sunflower County in the early period, but information became scarce later. I heard about Otis Brown's election campaign, but not about Charles McLaurin's subsequent bid to become a state senator or even the death of Fannie Lou Hamer until I read a book about her some years later.

It was Otis, who had moved to Connecticut, who first made contact, visiting me towards the end of the nineties. He was in his early fifties and I was close to sixty, but it was a great visit and it meant so much to me to see him so successful. Not long after that Karen mentioned that there was to be a thirty-fifth-anniversary reunion in Indianola in 1999. I considered going, but couldn't fit it in with my school schedule that year. But following that reunion Otis contacted me about a second reunion for the next year. Karen was so excited about the first one it was contagious and I agreed to go. I talked to John and he said he would go too. My daughter Rachel, a history major, also wanted to go and see for herself some living history.

On June 2, 2000, she and I got to the Memphis airport and then waited until John's plane arrived from Birmingham. The three of us rented a car and left for Mississippi in the late afternoon. We picked up Interstate 55 outside the airport and drove for two hours along this highway, new since the last time I was in the state. Outside Winona, where Mrs. Hamer had been savagely beaten thirty-seven years earlier, we picked up Highway 82. We drove then to Indianola, but were too late for the registration so we got our rooms at the Holiday Inn. Black hotel clerks kindly greeted us in a place they never would have been allowed inside in 1965. We got directions to the B.B. King concert that was to be in a park near Main Street, not far from the Indianola jail. We parked and joined the festive crowd coming to hear him.

The crowd was totally integrated and white sat next to black, both cheering King and his music. I would encounter many other changes in the weekend, but this integrated crowd, who loved B.B. King so much, was the biggest surprise of the reunion. My mind went back to his concerts at the all-black Club Ebony where he bought us chicken dinners. King made an effort to get both white and black children on the stage with him for some of his songs, and one could see the satisfaction in the seventy-five-year-old's eyes as he succeeded. It was a long way from the early fifties, when he sang on Church Street.

The next morning there was a bus tour of Sunflower County, where we saw among other places the Drew jail, now dilapidated and overgrown with weeds. In Ruleville the new black mayor gave us a welcome speech and we went to the gravesite of Fannie Lou Hamer,

Reunion at the Drew Jail: from left to right: Fred Winn, Jim Dann, Linda Davis, Charles McLaurin, Chris Hexter, Mike Yarrow and John Harris on the far right.

which is well kept with marble stones. In the afternoon we had a plenary session. Among the attendees on that bus ride or the plenary were Dale Gronemeir, Herschel Kaminsky, Karen Koonan, Len Edwards, Otis Brown, Cephus Smith, Linda Davis and Fred Winn.

There was a greeting from the white mayor of Indianola and the black state senator, followed by some kind of panel discussion, in the middle of which Charles McLaurin arrived. It was an emotional reunion for both of us. He recounted to the audience how I had driven him off the highway at a hundred miles an hour one day trying to avoid being passed. He at that point had a position as assistant director of public works for Indianola. Of the attendees both Linda Davis and Len Edwards were judges, he in San Jose, she in DC. Dale Gronemeir was then practicing law in Los Angeles.

One of the panelists was Zellie Rainey Orr who had been one of the eight- or nine-year-olds who had bravely been part of the library bust. She and the other little kids had held their own and never broke ranks even after all the adults and high school kids had been taken away to jail. She later went on to be in the first class that integrated the white school in Indianola, another act of courage. She became a published poet in Atlanta and at some point met and married Charles Scattergood. He, unfortunately, later died in a car accident. She was instrumental in getting a new housing project in Indianola named after Scattergood, which was dedicated to him, and his sister was present at the dinner that evening.

At the evening banquet I saw Thelma Mack, and when I asked about Cora Fleming she told me she had died. That was sad news. At the next reunion in 2004 I found out that Thelma Mack had herself died in the interim. In 2000 I also saw Alice Giles, who told me that her husband, Oscar Giles, had died since last we saw each other. Many things happen when you are out of touch for thirty-five years.

Most interesting to me was meeting the two young editors of the *Enterprise-Tocsin*, the newspaper that had spent so much time libeling me and others in that earlier period. These young white guys had taken charge of the paper some years back and converted it from a reactionary rag into a progressive voice and a fine example of small-town journalism. They were most sympathetic to us and their coverage of the reunion was kind and generous. They were examples of the positive changes that had affected Sunflower County in the thirty-five years since I had left. The many black elected and appointed officials in local government were another example and what seemed to me most important of all in that short visit was a genuine desire of younger white people (under forty) to overcome the past prejudices and racist practices of the older generation.

On the Sunday morning of the reunion I was surprised when the reporter for the *Enterprise-Tocsin* came to me and John and said that ex-Sheriff Hollowell wanted to meet the two of us. John demurred, saying he had nothing to say to Hollowell; I understood that sentiment very well but was curious anyway and, accompanied by Fred Winn, went to a nearby café and had coffee with Bill Hollowell, then a frail man probably close to eighty. I asked him what he had done in the intervening years and he related that he had achieved his ambition to become an FBI agent after his term as sheriff, but for some reason that job didn't work out well and he returned to Mississippi to become warden of the state prison at Parchman, where he ended his career. I asked him about Parker; Hollowell told me that Parker was still an inveterate racist, kept to himself and was very bitter about the way things worked out. He was implying that he, Hollowell, was happy with, or at least reconciled to, majority black rule.

Hollowell was trying then, and in an earlier interview I had read in the local paper, to project the image that he had been professional as a sheriff, above the fray and always out to protect us civil rights workers from harm, even if he disagreed with our tactics. Frankly, I could hardly credit that self-view, but did not argue with him on the point at the time. It might now be charitable to grant him this self-image given that he has since died, but it would not at all accord with the facts. A professional sheriff would have at the very least tracked down and arrested the violent white criminals who during his tenure had preyed upon civil rights workers in the county; those culprits were either known to him or their identities could have been discovered with little trouble. Nor was he there "when we needed him." His idea of himself as someone who protected us was self-delusion at best. We survived the year mostly due to the support of the black people of the county who looked after us and protected us from harm; we also carefully observed all the precautions taught us in the training and by McLaurin; the pressure from our friends in the North and the ubiquitous lawyers had some effect, and finally to some extent we were just lucky. No thanks are due to Hollowell nor to his FBI buddies who indeed may have wished us no harm, but did nothing practical to protect us.

More important was his failure to protect the black people, and especially those who had tried to register to vote, from the arsons, shootings and bombings. The loss of Irene Magruder's house was a serious and irreparable blow to her and her family as was the burning of the Sunflower church to the black community of that town. The shooting of the two young girls at the Sisson house and the burning of the Freedom School were examples of crimes that a "professional" sheriff should have pursued with vigor and intensity. Hollowell never showed the slightest interest in either prevention or prosecution of these crimes against the black majority of citizens in the county.

That said, however, his retrospective attitude toward the period was indicative of a sea change in how at least many whites viewed blacks. It was a sign of the change in attitude that he even cared so much. For most whites the condescension and even violent assertion of racial superiority had given way to acceptance of at least civil equality and in daily life there was now some level of decency that was very new and good to see.

But the situation was complex; not everything that happened in the thirty-five years happened for the best. There were in some other aspects no significant changes. When the courts in 1969 finally forced the schools of Indianola to integrate, the white power structure was ready. A new all-white Indianola Academy, supposedly a private school and thus beyond the civil rights law, opened its doors simultaneously with the integration of the public school. The decision to integrate came down on a Friday; on the next Monday not a single white student showed up at the public school and all of them went to the white academy. The end result throughout the county within a year or two was an all-black public school system, starved for funds from a school board still controlled by the white power structure, and all-white academies, flushed with cash from who knows where. By and large this was the situation in education at every level and in all places in the county.

The former downtown of Indianola with its Piggly-Wiggly, gun shops and "key club" was now all boarded up and abandoned, but also once-thriving businesses in the black community, like the White Rose Café and the Giles Penny Saver Store, had also disappeared. The exception was Club Ebony, kept alive thanks no doubt to the financial support of B.B. King. The center of commerce had shifted to Highway 82 with its huge Walmart, and some chain restaurants and motels, which made it impossible for any local merchants in either the formerly white or black areas of town to compete. Poverty was everywhere and there was little sign that civil rights had brought much in the way of economic rights to blacks. When one left Indianola for Sunflower or Drew the poverty was, if anything, considerably worse than in the sixties. Both towns, already in decline in 1965, had lost most of their population since then and both now have a forty percent poverty rate; they have visibly skidded further into a morass of hopeless penury. The once dominant cotton plantations had largely given way to huge catfish farms, which had at that time a ready export market in Asia. But these operations could make do with much less labor than cotton plantations and this development contributed to the endemic black unemployment, which was only a little relieved by blacks being hired by Walmart, local government, and the hotel chains from which they had formerly been excluded.

The reunion had largely been organized by Stacy White, a dynamic great-niece of Irene Magruder, who had died some time before. Stacy, an Associate Professor at Mississippi Valley State, was enthusiastic, warm, engaging and welcoming. There was a genuine desire on the part of her and others to preserve the history of the struggle in the county and a Black Historical Society had been founded and headquartered in Ruleville. The commemorative gravesite of Mrs. Hamer was also a step in the struggle to preserve the history. The sign entering Ruleville said: "Home to Fannie Lou Hamer." Naturally Charles McLaurin played a big role in guiding the younger people in the effort to keep alive the history. The 2000 reunion was also an important page in this history.

The three of us drove to Memphis on Sunday. John had an early plane to Birmingham and Rachel and I visited the Blues Museum in Memphis while waiting for our flight back to California. It was June 4, 2000.

Four years later Stacy White organized another reunion, August 5-7, 2004. This time I met John in Birmingham. He was hosting a visit with his daughter Pamela and her wife Carolina and the four of us on August 5 got in a rented car and drove to Indianola together. The drive took about five hours. Alabama and especially the Birmingham area has prospered in the last forty years in a way that the Mississippi Delta has not. It was very striking to see the contrast when one crossed the border between the two states. A diverse economy in both industrial and agricultural sectors has taken root in Alabama, while Mississippi has not only been unable to attract industry, but also its agricultural monocrop economy—formerly of cotton, now largely catfish—seems to have stagnated. Casinos in the Gulf Coast and Greenville provide some income and jobs, but are a poor substitute for value-creating production. The economic legacy of the racist-terrorist state of the sixties weighs heavily today, even after blacks achieved a large measure of civil equality.

In Sunflower County we were to see the full measure of the electoral progress that the black residents had achieved. By 2004 almost every elected official in the county was now black. And from what we could see they were progressive and honest people who were intent on doing the best for the people of the county in a way that is extremely rare in American civic life. At a luncheon on Saturday we were addressed by Bennie Thompson, who now represents the second congressional district in the House. He is one of the most progressive congressmen in the House and his stirring speech to us was a high point of the reunion. The fact that this district could go from being represented by an arch-reactionary like Jamie Whitten to such a sterling representative of the best in American politics is a signal success of the civil rights movement. And it made me proud to have played some small role in that struggle. Unfortunately, on the statewide level right-wing Republicans dominate and although very polite to the black citizens of the state compared to what we saw in 1964-65 they enforce policies that do little good for the black people and keep the state from progressing.

By contrast Alabama, which also is run by arch-reactionary Republicans, put a large campus of their university in Birmingham, a majority black city. They invested heavily in the University of Alabama at Birmingham, which has now become the leading medical center in the Deep South. John Harris was employed by the University as a psych tech for almost twenty years. The establishment of the University brought a measure of prosperity to all the city's citizens, black and white, and established many paths for skilled and technical jobs for young blacks. The campus also drew many liberal and progressive-minded whites as well as other minorities into the city as students and faculty, which augurs well for the future of the city and increases the chances for meaningful integration and a diverse cultural life. Mississippi did nothing of the sort for its majority black areas, choosing instead a policy of neglect and casino building. The jobs at the river casinos or

Walmart don't offer blacks the opportunities for education and advancement of skills that the University of Alabama at Birmingham medical school does. The contrast between Birmingham and Sunflower County was striking.

On August 6 a ceremony was held to dedicate three historical markers that were put up by the Mississippi Department of Archives and History. One was for the March 5, 1965, firebombing of the Freedom School; the other two for the May 1 firebombings that led to the destruction of the Magruder house and the serious damage to the Giles Penny Saver Store. The Sunflower Black Historical Society worked very hard with Zellie Orr's Charles Scattergood Foundation to arrange for these from the state, but had to pay for them; of course; the state of Mississippi wouldn't even attempt to make amends for its crimes of the sixties and at least pay for the markers. John and I, along with Linda Davis, Otis, Herschel, Karen, Fred and others paid for the Freedom School plaque. The Giles Store marker was paid for by the Giles family and the Magruder Home marker by her family. The state just lent its imprimatur to the event and we in turn were addressed by Elbert Hilliard, the director of the state's Department of History, who in his speech said of the burnings that the events "are about the worst period in our history." Pure sophistry! In fact these events of 1965 typified one hundred and fifty years of Mississippi history. If the Mississippi Department of History were to commemorate all the lynchings, murders, church burnings and more in the sad history of that state there wouldn't be enough copper in all the mines of Montana to make the plaques. Later that day we visited the site of the Emmett Till lynching, and I didn't notice any historical marker there. I suppose Till's mother couldn't afford to pay for one.

The hypocrisy of the state government aside, it was an important and very uplifting event to see these plaques and to see the courage and determination of Irene Magruder and Oscar Giles given the honor and distinction they so richly deserved. Alice Giles was there and the pride in her face was unmistakable; the same was true of

The dedication of a marker at the site of Mrs. Magruder's House was in 2004. Stacy White, her great-niece, is fourth from the left. Stacy did more than anyone else to keep the memory of the Indianola Movement alive. She indefatigably organized all the reunions and put together a brochure and driving tour of Indianola. She is now President of the Sunflower County Civil Rights Organization. L. to r.: John Harris, Jim Dann, Wilton White, Mrs. Magruder's grandson, Stacy White, her great niece, Alan Cooper. The seventh person from the left is Marsha-White Lloyd, another great niece.

the Magruder children and relatives, especially Stacy White, who had worked tirelessly so that the memory of Irene Magruder would never fade. John Harris appropriately spoke at the Magruder dedication since he was the first to stay at her house: "She was the first of many brave, honest people in Indianola to offer their houses to us... Mrs. Magruder had a great determination—a determination that 'We shall overcome. We shall defeat these people.'"

Otis was the principal speaker at the dedication of the Freedom School: "Even though it was bombed it gave us hope and that hope is still alive." Otis, at seventeen, had been the star student of the Freedom School, and nobody could speak to the hope it had engendered better than he. The speaker at the Giles dedication was Robert

In 2000 Ruleville had established a small gravesite for Fannie Lou Hamer. By 2012 there was a statue of her and an appropriately elaborate memorial in a park, nicely kept up, adjacent to the old black section of Ruleville. The sign leading from the highway proclaims: "Ruleville Home to Fannie Lou Hamer." It is often a mark of historical greatness that leaders, who were reviled during their lifetime, are widely honored posthumously, a fate shared with Hamer by both Abraham Lincoln and Martin Luther King.

Merritt, who as a neighbor had witnessed the bombing and helped put out the fire. He eventually became Indianola school superintendent when majority rule finally came to Indianola. Oscar Giles would have been proud of his neighbor's achievement. Besides Alice Giles, her son, her daughter (whom I used to bounce on my knee), her son-in-law and her grandchild witnessed the dedication with pride.

Not many more than a hundred people were present, mostly veterans of the movement or their relatives; tellingly, except for the reporters not a single white county resident came. We subsequently all piled onto two buses that took us on a tour of other civil rights sites in the county. McLaurin led the tour. Besides the Hamer gravesite and the obligatory stop and photo op at the Drew jail we went to Sunflower where we saw the Sunflower Freedom Project.

Tracy Sugarman and John Harris reunited in 2004. Much more important to the Sunflower movement than an excellent journalist and renowned illustrator, Tracy lived with us in Ruleville and shared weal and woe with the volunteers. His maturity and love for the participants was an important stabilizing force while he was there. Later in Westport, CT, he organized a support network without which the volunteers never would have survived the winter.

In an old abandoned storefront on the other side of Annie Mae King's old house (since burned down—accidentally) a group of young people from the North, who had come to the county in 1994 as part of the Teach for America Program, had set up an academy in 1998 to tutor young high school kids, enrich their cultural program, add classes they were not getting in school and encourage them to go to college. They bought the abandoned storefront in 2002. This program had great success and their "fellows," about forty in number who have stuck with the program, have each and every one graduated high school, usually near the top of their class and gone on to a four-year college. Students starting at grade seven are drawn not only from that impoverished town, but also from the failing public schools in Ruleville, Indianola, Moorhead and Leland. The program runs during the school year, including Saturdays, and has an intensive summer program as well as field trips to colleges and civil rights and Civil War sites. The summer programs are called "Freedom Schools" and are inspired by the Freedom Schools of our era. The program is demanding and has an important component teaching the history of the civil rights movement in Sunflower County. It meant a lot to me personally to see such a needed program doing so much for the local kids and located just across the vacant lot where I once lived for six months now forty years in the past. Even the teachers at the school had not been born then and the students they are tutoring may well be the grandkids of some of the young people who kept me company, protected me and helped organize that town. I have kept up with the school since 2004 and from its newsletter have learned of its success stories.

At this reunion I renewed contact with old friends I hadn't seen in forty years. Mike Yarrow, Dennis Flannigan and Chris Hexter, who were in our original group of voter registration volunteers, came to the reunion and seemed to be doing well. Rabbi Allan Levine came all the way from Israel to join the reunion. Liz Fusco, who had set up the Freedom Schools in both Indianola and Ruleville came too; she has been in education since, I think in Connecticut. The late Tracy Sugarman then over eighty also came and was actively researching his second book on that freedom summer and its aftermath, *We Had Sneakers, They Had Guns.* He showed me his excellent first book, *Strangers at the Gate,* and interviewed me and John for the second book. When I got home I ordered the earlier book as well as two other books he had written and illustrated about other topics. We were very fortunate to have had such a group of dedicated, intelligent, talented and morally exemplary volunteers with us that first summer. I learned to appreciate that fact much more during the reunions possibly than I had at the time.

Tracy interviewed John and me in the library, a beautiful building. To think that in 1964 so many people had to be arrested for it to be used by the black citizens of the county. The library had a display of Tracy's drawings from that freedom summer, on loan from Tougaloo College, where they are permanently housed. The librarian, a white lady about forty, was most sympathetic and very interested in our accounts of that year in Mississippi.

At the banquet Lawrence Guyot was the main speaker. He was as articulate as ever and both he and McLaurin told of the first times they came to the Delta. The courage of those first young men to come to Ruleville in those days still never ceases to astound me. Guyot was still very active in politics and friends with Bennie Thompson. I had seen him once on Fox News debating Bill O'Reilly. Guyot could easily hold his own against that shrill reactionary. The upcoming election of Bush vs. Kerry was a big topic and Guyot even held out hope that with a big black turnout Mississippi would vote for Kerry and give the state to Kerry. (It didn't happen.)

The next day back we drove to Alabama and in Birmingham I left John, Pamela and Carolina and caught a plane for Sacramento. I had had a good time at the reunion and was happy to hear that in 2008 another one was scheduled.

John, however, decided not to attend in 2008. So my wife Arley and I flew to Birmingham to visit with him for a few days, enjoy the wonderful Civil Rights Museum in that city and then drive to Indianola. This reunion was timed to coincide with the opening of the B.B. King Museum in Indianola. The grand opening was attended by about four hundred people in an area near the park where we had heard King play in 2000. The crowd was largely integrated, as was the podium, where Carver Randle—Bridges's brother and now a successful attorney—co-chaired with a white lady, whom I gathered was the wife of a plantation owner. The local black politicians shared the stage with the white statewide politicians, including the lieutenant governor. It was interesting that B.B. King could bring out such an integrated group, while civil rights memorials could not. Still, the white and black together to honor B.B. King and his music was a sign of just how far Mississippi had traveled. There were two marching bands to entertain the crowd; one was all-black from Mississippi Valley State, the other all-white from some white academy, a sign of how far the state still had to go in school desegregation. The museum was state-of-the art; very modern, interactive and informative and the gift shop and outside vendors did a brisk business in souvenirs and t-shirts. The hope is that some tourism from the buses on their way to casinos by the river will make a stop in Indianola and drop a few dollars into the local economy.

The reunion itself the night before was sparsely attended. The low turnout was no fault of Stacy White, who had worked tirelessly to promote and organize the event. There was a conflict with a B.B. King concert. As always, Charles McLaurin led the proceedings and was very welcoming. The high point of the dinner was a speech by John Lewis, who gave a very inspiring talk to all of us. The election campaign being in full swing, it absorbed all of our attention and the majority of Lewis's remarks were for all of us to work hard for Barack Obama. There was even some hope expressed at the reunion that the state of Mississippi might vote for Obama since it was forty percent black and if only about one fifth of the white voters voted for Obama he could carry the state. But outside the reunion the people seemed to have little hope of that outcome. At the B.B. King ceremony I was wearing an Obama t-shirt and a black vendor asked me where I was from, since she felt that no white Mississippians would ever wear one. Later that afternoon when I checked in at the Birmingham, Alabama, hotel wearing the same t-shirt, the white desk clerk, a college kid at University of Alabama at Birmingham, said he was going to get an Obama t-shirt for himself, another sign of the growing cultural gap between Birmingham and Sunflower County.

The project of President Johnson and Hodding Carter to establish an integrated but white-run Democratic Party in Mississippi had by this time come to an inglorious end. The white Democratic office holders over the years felt they had to adopt increasingly conservative positions to appeal to white voters, while taking the black vote for granted. But whites were switching to the more stridently reactionary Republican Party, preferring the real thing as opposed to the pale reflection offered by the white Democrats, who go by the name "Blue Dog Democrats"; the origin of that name is obscure but reflects their lack of principles. Progressive blacks increasingly won more and more offices in the state, while the Blue Dogs faded away. The last of them were drummed out of majority-white districts in 2010, and they will not be missed. So now in Mississippi (and in Alabama, Georgia and South Carolina) there is a very progressive black Democratic Party with many more black elected officials than in most northern states, exemplified by congressmen Bennie Thompson and John Lewis, on the one hand, and an extremely reactionary, corrupt and intellectually barren Republican Party, exemplified by Governor Haley Barbour, who recently went so far as to state that he didn't remember any racial problems in the sixties, on the other hand.

In the end of course, Obama carried none of these states as too few Deep South white voters could bring themselves to vote for him. (He did, however, carry the more modern states of North Carolina, Virginia and Florida.) The campaign of 2008 and its outcome were a big victory for the civil rights movement and all we fought for in 1964-65. While we were at the reunion the polls showed a temporary advantage for John McCain, the Republican candidate. But as the campaign proceeded, in short order McCain showed his utter ineptitude for the office, Obama's principles resonated with the voters and his clear intellectual superiority became manifest to most people. The campaign was not unlike Goldwater's bid in 1964, the only other Arizonan to run for President. Like his predecessor, McCain and especially his moronic running mate, Sarah Palin, resorted to strident, thinly disguised racism as their only hope of turning the tide. But the country had come a long way since 1964 and the decisive victory of Obama was a great inspiration to us all.

Since the election unrepentant racists organized by Fox News and well funded by billionaire haters have founded the "Tea Party" (an insult to the Boston Patriots of 1774) to try to reverse the trend of 2008. The rallies of this group of angry, mostly older people with little sense of reality resemble in no small way the mobs of young racists that used to attack civil rights marchers. Perhaps many of them are the same people only forty years older or their children, ill brought up.

But that motley crew is a reflection of an ugly past. The last city we passed through in leaving Mississippi was Columbus, where in 1964 McLaurin and four friends were subjected to a savage beating by highway patrolmen; the sadistic cops would not stop until the civil rights workers would tell them they were "niggers." We stopped for lunch in that town in 2008 and in a nice trendy café we were greeted and waited on by a completely integrated group of young people in their twenties, black and white, working side by side and obviously fully at ease with each other. This is the future of Mississippi.

Afterword by John Harris

It seems like the White Citizens' Council and the Ku Klux Klan were sometimes not really organized. I guess they thought with some arrests during the summer they could wait for us to leave and things might be the same as before. Things changed for us because the project was intended to be a summer project, but things change. Some of the 1961 sit-ins were not intended to focus on Woolworths and Kress but did as changes occurred.

I think the volunteers saw the strength of the enemy over the summer but also the determination of the black people of Mississippi for change. The KKK was more able to hide their hoods and robes for a while but saw a strong enemy and increased their terror!

The KKK could easily see what was going on in Sunflower so they attacked the house where the freedom organizers lived. The freedom workers made a decision to defend themselves and their supporters. It was necessary. Not many local people were ready to take on changes in voting (registering) and challenging the KKK if they saw the organizers destroyed. I don't know how much our northern supporters were aware of the self-defense—but it was no secret in our environment and, of course, accepted by our supporters.

Since the November 1964 election was near, the Mississippi Freedom Democratic Party, the Council of Federated Organizations, the Student Nonviolent Coordinating Committee and the National Democratic Party were facing a decision of what to do about the MFDP challenge of the Mississippi congressmen, how to handle the Johnson candidacy and how to keep the struggle moving forward! There were some differences among some of the SNCC, MFDP people and the national Democrats. I'm not sure if the average civil rights supporter in Mississippi was deeply concerned about the November election, but many cast "freedom ballots" —of course, the average black voter in the Delta and Mississippi supported Johnson because he sounded more reasonable.

That trip to Tallahatchie County to find the Moorhead woman who owned a building to possibly hold a voter mass meeting was another experience that can't be forgotten—even though it's not talked about much. It's good we had the two-way radio in some of the cars we used. While "playing around" with the radio we heard a conversation that we had been spotted and they planned to stop us at any time in a short distance. Our senses told us this was dangerous. With Jim's reaction behind the wheel (quick and fast) we got out of there and made it back to Ruleville. Sometimes we all experience some luck—that was a case of extremely good luck and steady and fast driving.

Of course Goldwater won the popular vote in Mississippi and about five other states.

The people's defense of the Sunflower church was another example of some people taking a stand for what's right, the right of the people to hold freedom meetings in the church. There were threats. Basically the people's defense team at the church, which had rifles to defend the building, came out after the deputies surrounded the church; the SNCC staff negotiated to empty the church and the deputies, who were scared, let our people out and negotiated a plea deal with Jim. It was the best deal to end the situation. When you are in some difficult and new daily situations, you play the hand you are dealt and hope things end as another learning experience.

Some of the facts and thoughts of this Sunflower experience could be useful for anyone involved in organizing in a new area or under a difficult challenge. Lots of heart goes into the situation, dedication to what you are doing, trying new things, learning from mistakes and a strong love for the people.

Some of the SNCC people moved on to Selma during the March '65 demonstrations there. It was a bigger and more visible series of events than the period of voter registration struggle in Mississippi. People were willing to work and support what was right. The signing of the Voting Rights Act in 1965, the rebellions of black citizens and their supporters in cities around the country, the women's liberation movement and the gay rights movement were all challenges and I believe most of us who spent time organizing in Mississippi benefited and passed on the lessons to others and will never forget what happened.

John HARRIS, Birmingham, Alabama, May 14, 2011

Appendix –
Organizations and Civil Rights
Leaders Referred to

....

1. **SNCC**- Student Nonviolent Coordinating Committee: Founded in 1960 after the initial sit-in movement by a conference of black student leaders of the sit-in movement. It was the major organization in the Mississippi summer project. It disappeared during the early seventies.

2. **SCLC**- Southern Christian Leadership Conference: Founded in 1957 after the Montgomery Bus Boycott by Dr. Martin Luther King and sixty other black ministers. This group led most of the major civil rights struggles in Alabama and Georgia from 1957 until 1966. It provided some support for the Mississippi project, but ceded leadership to SNCC. The organization is largely inactive now.

3. **CORE**- Congress of Racial Equality: Founded in 1941 in northern cities and mainly active in desegregation in large urban centers, particularly Chicago. It originated the idea of the Freedom Rides in 1961 and eventually established a presence in central Mississippi and in Louisiana. It worked closely with SNCC, but in a secondary role in the summer project. The organization veered to the right in the seventies and has disappeared since then.

4. **NAACP**- National Association for the Advancement of Colored People: Founded in 1909 in the aftermath of the Springfield, Illinois, mob riot that lynched and burned out the blacks of that town, it became the leading civil rights organization in the United States. Banned in much of the Deep South during the fifties with a number of leaders murdered, it lost influence and footing in that area and many NAACP members in Mississippi worked under SNCC's leadership after 1963. The national organization gave little support to the summer project. It is still active today, mainly in voter registration efforts.

5. **COFO**- Council of Federated Organizations: Founded in 1962 as a coalition of the above four groups; it was the official sponsor of the summer project. It was dissolved in 1965.

6. **MFDP**- Mississippi Freedom Democratic Party: Founded in 1964 as an alternative to the all-white Democratic Party, it was the electoral organization of black Mississippians to challenge the racist system. It took over from the Council of Federated Organizations in 1965, but by the end of the decade had merged with the regular democrats, who by that time were forced to allow black participation.

7. **John Lewis** (b. 1940) was chairman of SNCC from 1960-1967. He was based in Atlanta, but lent crucial public leadership to the summer project. He has been a congressman from Georgia since 1987.

8. **James Forman** (1928-2005) was executive secretary of SNCC from 1961 to 1967. He was the most influential leader of the Mississippi project after Bob Moses.

9. **Bob Moses** (b. 1935) was the director of the Mississippi summer project and of COFO. He started the voter registration campaign in that state in 1962 and conceived and organized the summer project. He withdrew from leadership in 1965-66. In 1982 he returned with an Algebra project to improve math education in Mississippi.

10. **Dr. Martin Luther King** (1929-1968) was the leader of the Montgomery Bus Boycott and soon became the public leader of the civil rights movement. His unquestioned integrity, great intelligence, exemplary courage and peerless oratorical skills made him the most important American leader of this century. He was assassinated in 1968; a lone gunman took the rap but he was probably part of a larger conspiracy that has never been revealed.

A Short Note on Sources

··

The primary source of this essay is simply my memories; since John Harris was involved in most of these incidents I checked with him to verify the details of which he had knowledge. Of events that we were not directly part of, but which affected us, or to recall specific dates and names I have forgotten, I list sources that I consulted below. In addition it seemed necessary to give some historical background to understand the situation in Mississippi in 1964-65. Below I also list these sources. If not specifically cited below the source for the account above is simply my memory, verified where possible by John Harris. I apologize for any errors or omissions if others remember things differently. Please send criticisms, corrections, additions and comments to me care of info@barakabooks.com.

1. Chapter 1—A Trip from Los Angeles to Ohio: The history of the Reconstruction largely comes from DuBois's work, *Black Reconstruction*. An interesting article on Adelbert Ames on Wikipedia was helpful.

2. Chapter 2—The Training in Oxford, Ohio: My memories of that week were supplemented by the keen observations of Tracy Sugarman in his book, *Strangers at the Gates*. The history of the idea of the summer project, the Voter Education Project, Medgar Evers and the Council of Federated Organizations largely comes

from the long on-line article on the principal civil rights struggles in the South, *Veterans of the Civil Rights Movement-Timeline,* (http://crmvet.org/tim), which was written by a number of SNCC, CORE and other civil rights workers after lengthy seminars in which they collectively discussed their memories. It is by far the most detailed, unbiased and authoritative source on the Southern civil rights movement 1951-1964.

3. Chapter 3—Our Base in Ruleville: The lynching of Michael Schwerner, James Chaney and Andrew Goodman is covered well in the *Veterans of the Civil Rights Movement-Timeline* cited above. For details of the involvement of high state officials in that murderous plot and its cover-up see the article by Ben Chaney in *Human Rights Magazine,* Spring 2000. Some details that I forgot about the first days in Ruleville are in Tracy Sugarman's book cited above. Some of the early history of the Ruleville civil rights movement is from *Ruleville-Civil Rights Driving Tour,* published in February 2008 by the Hamer Institute at Jackson State University. The article by Chris Wren in *Look,* September 8, 1964, was also helpful.

4. Chapter 4—The Standoff in Drew: The second and third rallies as well as the meeting in Mound Bayou are well covered by Tracy Sugarman both in the book cited above and in his second book, *We Had Sneakers, They Had Guns.* All incidents that summer were reported to SNCC headquarters in Atlanta and compiled as WATS reports, some of which were printed verbatim in the appendix to *Freedom Summer* by Doug McAdam. The events in Drew July 14-15 are covered in these WATS reports. Both sources accord with my memory as well; the exact quotations from John Harris and Charles McLaurin at the rallies are from Sugarman, who witnessed these events.

5. Chapter 5—Breakthrough in Indianola: The events at the Atlantic City convention are covered best in the *Veterans of the Civil Rights Movement-Timeline.* But also for the manipulations of Johnson, Humphrey, Moyers *et al.* see John Dittmer, *Local People,* who used

as sources testimony from the Senate Watergate investigation. John Lewis in his autobiography, *Walking with the Wind,* also reinforces these accounts. The language and slurs against Hamer by President Johnson and Vice-President Humphrey, which are quoted in the footnote, were taken verbatim from an account by Ed King, an eyewitness to the event, which he reported to a February 11, 2000, panel discussion, Atlantic City Revisited, hosted by ex-Vice-President Walter Mondale. Neither Mondale (who had been Johnson's chief representative on the 1964 credentials committee) nor the other panelists, all participants in the events, disputed the account or Humphrey's language. The Monroe, North Carolina, incident is also from *Veterans of the Civil Rights Movement-Timeline.* See *Indianola, Civil Rights History Driving Tour* by the Hamer Institute for the incident about Slim Jack and locations of various Indianola sites. The B.B. King Museum in Indianola has a good display about the blues scene in Indianola in the early fifties.

6. Chapter 6—The Autumn Desegregation Offensive in Indianola: The Lowenstein meeting and SNCC's reaction to it are from Dittmer's *Local People.* The Weber Restaurant bust is described in the WATS report of October 4, 1964, and that is why I have all the names. Other actions described were all from personal memory and discussions with John Harris, and we can't remember exactly who was arrested in which incident.

7. Chapter 7—The Klan Strikes Back: The tension between MFDP and SNCC is described in Dittmer's *Local People.* Also consulted was a COFO press release of October 29, 1964, for the events of October 28-29.

8. Chapter 8—A Winter to Keep On Pushing: See Wikipedia, *Ku Klux Klan,* for its history. The background to the Waveland meeting and tensions within SNCC are from Dittmer's *Local People.* A COFO press release of December 26, 1964, which I kept, gives details of the Christmas attacks on us in Sunflower. The events in Selma are best described in John Lewis's *Walking with the Wind.*

9. Chapter 9—New Hopes and New Paths of Struggle: The background to the founding of the Child Development Group of Mississippi and its relation with the Office of Economic Opportunity is from Dittmer, who had access to Levin's papers.

10. Chapter 10—Return to Mississippi: See *Enterprise-Tocsin* of June 8, 2000, and August 12, 2004. Also consulted were the brochures by the Sunflower County Black Historical Association for each of the three reunions. For information on the Sunflower Freedom Project see their website. Information on the Indianola Academy and population/poverty rates in Sunflower County are from two Wikipedia entries under those names. The Civil Rights Museum in Birmingham is one of the best historical museums in the world—better in my opinion than the Smithsonian in DC and most museums in Europe; it is a must-see if you are ever in the South.

Acknowledgements

A book like this, the story of a mass movement, owes much to all the people involved, residents of Sunflower County and the volunteers who traveled down there in 1964, all of whom so impacted my memories. But above all two men, John Harris and Charles McLaurin, had the most direct effect on the book.

I never would have had this manuscript published but for the enthusiastic, unstinting and warm encouragement of Charles McLaurin. At every step of the process he was supportive of me, just like he had been in other ways in Mississippi fifty years ago. He generously contributed many of the illustrations, but mainly it was his constant encouragement that kept me going.

My children, James, Michael, and Rachel were my first audience; they listened to these stories in the car and on vacations. I was just trying to keep them from being bored till we got to our destination, but they genuinely looked forward to the next "chapters" and years later asked me to write them down.

The manuscript then had been privately circulated among family and close friends. Tracy Sugarman was the first person to tell me to find a publisher. Given his prolific output as an author, I was flattered and for the first time took the prospect seriously. He had previously been kind enough to give me some of his illustrations, which had helped jog my memory of some events, and his two excellent books on our Ruleville experience also filled in some blanks of times fifty years ago.

It was my old friend Phil Taylor who, after I gave an interview on his excellent Toronto radio show, asked for a copy of the manuscript and acted on my behalf to find a publisher.

Robin Philpot, Phil's friend, soon called me and surprised me by saying his firm, Baraka Books, would publish it. Robin patiently guided me through the new-to-me process, made many significant corrections and put up with my many revisions as for the first time I took the prospect of a wider readership seriously. Robin and Josée Lalancette, Baraka Books' production manager, did a wonderful job in designing the book and thought of many things that needed to be done. I never would have guessed how much work goes into designing and publishing a book. They thought that pictures and illustrations would do much to improve the book and make it understandable. So together we began a search for any pictures that might have survived the time. I had saved none.

Charles McLaurin let us use a number of Tracy Sugarman's drawings, which Tracy had given him. But for photos it was my friend Herschel Kaminsky, who found a treasure-trove of old photos he had taken during his time in Indianola. He gave unstintingly of his time to pore through old photographs to find ones that fit with this book. He then went to a lot of trouble to get them on discs and send them to me and Robin. These photos were never published before and have made a vast difference in the design of the book and its understandability. Herschel also kindly corrected some of my mistakes in the circulated manuscripts and helped me improve the book.

Otis Brown, like Charles McLaurin, was warm and encouraging from the first time he saw the manuscript. He helped identify some of the people in the illustrations as well as correcting some mistakes in the earlier version.

Mabel Giles Whitaker, the daughter of Alice and Oscar Giles, was kind enough to send me some material about her parents. Zellie

Orr also generously gave me some useful background material. Rachel Dann and Pamela Harris were kind enough to send me photos of the 2000 and 2004 reunions respectively. Thanks also to Rachel Dann, Pamela Harris, and Stacy White for providing photos of the reunion.

Stacy White, the unofficial resident historian of the Sunflower County Movement, was warm and encouraging to me from the first; she is great niece of Irene Magruder, who had been so crucial to our success in Indianola fifty years before. Stacy White made some very important corrections to both the text and the map of Indianola.

Arley Dann read each chapter as I wrote it and gave me enormous help in revising my rough style. Much more importantly she was a great critic and her critical eye was crucial in turning the first drafts from a self-centered account into something of more general interest.

John Harris was in many ways a virtual co-author. As I wrote a chapter I would send it to him and he would call me up. Often we spent up to an hour on the phone discussing the subject of that particular chapter and his input more than any other influence is reflected in the final product. John Harris was an activist to the end of his life and his input always reflected his chief concern, that our experiences in Mississippi fifty years ago be helpful to today's activists.

Jim DANN, June 2013

Publisher's Note

Jim Dann did me the honor of entrusting Baraka Books with his book entitled, *Challenging the Mississippi Firebombers, Memories of Mississippi 1964-65.* Our mutual friend, Phil Taylor of Toronto, told me that this would be an important book and that Jim was a great guy to work with. Although I never had the pleasure of meeting Jim and spoke to him only once on the phone, we enjoyed an intense—and for me, enriching—working relationship for a six-month period prior to publication. Never once did Jim let on that his health was anything but perfect until Friday, June 14, two days before he passed away. He worked extremely hard to make sure that this book would do justice to the courageous people of Mississippi and those who went there with him in 1964, as well as to the historic struggle they led. The first proofs were finished just days before Jim passed away. Until the end he did his job like the foot soldier he respected so much, Charles McLaurin of Indianola Mississippi. As his publisher, it is now our job to be the foot soldiers and to ensure the book enjoys the full prestige and reach it deserves. As we begin that work, Jim's devotion to the cause will be our guide and inspiration. Thank you Jim for everything.

Robin Philpot
Baraka Books.